Sunrise At Two Lions

Beautiful guru, master of the time, you came with just the perfect design. God of Love, Susan and Scoop, all children and friends who provided the clues, this one's for you.

Jeff Belyea

Portland, Maine
www.suiteonedesign.com

Sunrise At Two Lions

Published by
SuiteOne Design Group
Portland, Maine
www.suiteonedesign.com

ISBN 0-9720797-0-X
LCCN 2002092021

Contents

Forward

Introduction

Epilogue

Forward

Every once in a while a book comes along that has a spiritual story to tell and can complete it's mission with simplicity and grace. A story that doesn't tell you how to think, but opens your mind and quietly suggests you think for yourself instead.

Sunrise at Two Lions, is one of these books. A profoundly moving story about God's Grace and Love and how a young boy's life evolves after a unique experience with God. After a freak accident and a "near death experience" Billy, age 10, returns to life as "normal" with his family. His mother and father have trouble listening to his account of what happened, and his grandfather will hear nothing of it. It is up to his grandmother to quietly coax his experience from him and to help him cultivate and understand his new gift. Through life's ups and downs, Billy nearly forgets his gift, but finds the strength to reclaim it and the courage to begin sharing it with others.

Sunrise is a beautiful gem of a book that simply shares it's heart with the reader, and in the process opens the reader's heart a little bit wider.

from "Books Worth Reading" by P. Alan Stiles
on the web at www.wakingsouls.org

Introduction

I don't know these people. I don't know how much, if any, of this story is true. I only know what I heard from a fellow traveler, a storyteller, on an Amtrak train ride from Baltimore to Boston. This was a train ride that should have taken hours, yet in what seemed to be minutes, the ride was over and we pulled into South Station in Boston. It was as if something in the story, or in my own mind, had collapsed time.

When we came to a stop at the station, the storyteller handed me a thin little book. On each page in the book there was a poem and beside each poem there was an unusual painting. After looking through the book, I stood up to put it in my overcoat pocket. When I sat back down, the storyteller was gone. But his words were sealed in my mind and his book was in my pocket. So, I guess I am one of the storytellers. And now you have this book in your possession.

The story began in the nineteen-seventies, when a young boy from Maine was reported as missing in the dead of winter. Ninety days later, to the day, the boy who had been missing and given up for dead, was spotted just walking along the side of a country road. And, I am led to believe, told of a most amazing and inspiring adventure. The details of his episode and the incredible tale of what happened to him while he was missing; those that can be put into words, are contained within the story that you are about to read.

Jeff Belyea
jeff@mindgoal.com

Chapter One – Gone Fishing

"Billy, get up, your breakfast is getting cold." That was Nana Fraser's everyday wake–up call. A few seconds later she always added, "You better get up, Billy. You'll be late." But today she said, "Your Dad will be here any minute."

Nana always fudged about the time, just to get Billy in motion. And he knew it. But today, he bounced out of bed as soon as he heard Nana's voice. Billy was going ice fishing with his father. And Billy remembered how hungry he got out on the ice all day the last time they went. So he wanted to make sure he didn't miss breakfast today.

Two eggs, sunny side up, bacon, well done, dark toast, orange juice and a bowl of Corn Flakes, if he still had room, that was Billy's usual breakfast. It had been just about every day, since he came to live with his grandparents, four years before, when he was six years old.

Nana would set out his breakfast on the kitchen table just the way he liked it; bacon and eggs first, juice, toast and cereal second. Then she would open the door to the back stairs and call him to breakfast. Billy's room was right at the top of stairs. And Nana's high shrill voice was always amplified as it shot up the enclosed curved stairway and into Billy's room.

"BILLY!"

The second call could reach near eardrum-piercing levels. Billy was usually ready for it, with his ears covered. But this morning he didn't have to cover his ears, he was on his way down the stairs at first call.

"You better dress really warm, it's freezing cold," Nana said as Billy pulled his chair up to his morning banquet.

"Um–hum," he acknowledged through the half slice of toast he had already packed into his mouth in one bite.

"And slow down. You'll get a stomach ache."

"Um–hum."

Billy heard the Jeep pull into the driveway just as he was slurping the last few gulps of sweet milk from his cereal bowl. He dropped the bowl on the table, disappeared up the back stairs, and reappeared with his plastic tackle-box before the bowl had stopped spinning.

"Bye, Nan," he shouted back as he slammed the kitchen door, "Thanks for breakfast. See you tonight. Fish for dinner."

"You'll have to clean them first. Hey, you didn't say good-bye to Grampa."

Billy didn't answer back. He heard her, but he wasn't about to come back in and say good-bye to his grandfather. Too many times, Grampa had found an excuse at the last minute to ground Billy and ruin his plans. It happened a lot. So once Billy was out the door, he wasn't about to come back in. Anyway, Nana knew she'd end up cleaning the fish. She always did when Ron and Billy went fishing. And she knew why Billy hadn't said good-bye to Grampa, especially considering the fact that Billy's plans included Ron.

Ron, that's Billy's father, didn't come into the house. He never did. Billy's grandfather wouldn't allow it. But that's another story. Today, Billy's was going ice fishing.

"Hi, Dad," Billy chirped as tossed his tackle box in the back of the Jeep.

"Hey, Rascal, how you doing?"

"Rascal" was the nickname that Ron gave to Billy when he saw him for the very first time in the maternity ward at the hospital where Billy was born. Ron, Rachael and Rascal; that was the happy young King-Fraser family, at least for a few years.

Ron King and Rachael Fraser grew up across the street from each other up on Winter Hill in Gardiner, Maine. Rachael was a tomboy and she was just considered "one of the boys" by Ron, at least until they were older. Rachael could hit a baseball farther and run faster than most of the boys in the neighborhood until well into high school.

Ron was an easy-going kid, a mediocre student, usually a benchwarmer in sports, who skipped school a lot to go fishing as soon as the weather turned warm enough. That's early spring in Maine.

His father had been killed in a hunting accident when Ron was really young. Seems his father and a friend went out for pheasant one day. And as they walked across a field, one flew up. The friend wheeled around and fired off a shot at the bird. Problem was, Ron's father was standing between his friend and the bird.

So Ron grew up without a father around. He had a really good relationship with his mother, though. And she pretty much devoted her life to her son. She never had any more kids, and she was never remarried.

Ron promised himself that if he ever had children, he'd be sure that he stuck around to raise them. But that's not the way it turned out after he and Rachael got married. Now that was a real surprise to everybody.

It seemed liked overnight that things changed between Ron and Rachael. They were seniors in high school, still buddies, who hung out at each other's house like they had for years, listening to music, making snacks together, and emptying their family's respective refrigerators. Rachael would help Ron with studies, and Ron would listen, somewhat patiently, as Rachael would read out loud to him to help him finish an assigned book or prepare for a test.

The next thing anybody knew, out of the blue, they were talking about getting married. No one knew what happened all of a sudden, but there was plenty of speculation in the small, gossipy town.

Anyway, when Rachael's father heard about it, he went through the roof. He had, more than a few times, referred to Ron's family as, "good-for-nothing bums". Rachael had heard it and always just shrugged it off. But when she and Ron stood in front of her father and nonchalantly announced that they were talking about getting married, he exploded. He grabbed Ron by the arm and neck and literally threw him out of the house.

From that point on, Ron never came into Rachael's house. Ron and Rachael sneaked around to see each other for the rest of the school year. And, seven days out of high school, they took off together, and eloped.

They came back to Ron's house a few days later, on a Saturday. And Ron's mother took the news like it was no big deal at all. As soon as they told her what they had done, she reached over and gave Rachael a big hug, and asked them if they were going to live at home with her for a while. She was a very cool customer. It would not be the same reception at Rachael's house, not by a long shot.

Rachael called her mother from Ron's house and cheerfully announced that she and Ron had eloped. You could feel the anguish from across the street, let alone over the telephone.

"Your father will kill you." Rachael's mother whispered painfully into the phone. She always worried about her husband and his reactions, because he had such an explosive temper. She was always telling everybody in the family to keep their voice down, just in case they would inadvertently say anything to upset the old grouch.

"Where are you right now?" Nana demanded.

With that, and without a response, Rachael calmly hung up the phone and stormed across the street and into her house. Her father was in the living room watching a ballgame and he didn't even hear the door slam. Rachael's mother did, though, and she tried to stop Rachael from going into the living room. Her mother pleaded silently, shaking her head, but Rachael would not be stopped.

She was always a spitfire and more than a few times, growing up, let her father know that he wasn't going to bully her the way he did everyone else. She marched into the living room and stood between her father and the television. This was a definite no-no to begin with, so she really had her defiant face on. Before he could say a word, she blurted at him.

"Ronnie and I got married and if you don't like it, well, that's just too damn bad. I'm eighteen, and I'm out of here!"

Her father tried to respond. His face turned beet red, he gripped the sides of his chair like he was going to pounce, and then, to Rachael's stunned amazement, he broke down in tears.

Rachael had never seen her father show any signs of weakness, let alone tears. He was a tough boss, a tough husband and a tough disciplinarian. He never hit her, but he never hugged her either. She had never seen him so much as touch her mother. But here he was, with tears coming down his face. She didn't know what to do. But that didn't last long. In the next instant, her father's eyes turned cold, his jaw clenched, and he actually spit the words out at her.

"Get out of my sight."

"Fine with me!"

They didn't speak to each other until two years later, when

Billy was born, and after much pleading from Rachael's mother. In the hospital, the sight of Billy absolutely melted Rachael's father.

He still wouldn't even acknowledge Ron, but his faced softened for a quick instant and he actually reached over and touched his daughter's arm as she held Billy. Rachael and her father never really connected closely, but at least there was civility between them, again.

Six years later, Ron and Rachael decided to separate. Ron was a stick-in-the-mud and Rachael was full of energy. The resentment between them was beginning to show, and they each knew it. So, quietly and amicably, they worked out the terms of a divorce. And, not surprisingly, they were able to stay friends. They even laughed and joked about how they were much better friends than they were marriage partners.

Rachael had always wanted to travel, see Europe and the rest of the world. But Ron didn't want Billy to be away from him for long periods of time. So that's how Billy came to live with his grandmother and grandfather.

It was only supposed to be for a few weeks while Rachael traveled. But she quickly learned to love her freedom and the ability to move around whenever she wanted. And Nana liked having someone to wait on besides the old grouch.

So, with Billy off fishing with his father, Nana started cleaning up the kitchen. She stopped to put more coffee on and hollered to Grampa to ask if he wanted a warm up. It was a Saturday morning, so he was home from work. No answer. She kicked her voice up to that shrill and tried one more time.

"Grampa, you want a warm up?"

The old grouch was in his chair in the living room watching the morning news, and he had heard Billy and Nana talking. A lot of times Grampa would bellow from the living room and ask whoever was talking in the kitchen what they were whispering about. Other times you could yell in his ear and he'd make believe he didn't hear you. No one really believed he was all that hard of hearing, so they were usually pretty careful about what they said – especially about Grampa.

"For God sakes, you don't have to yell so loud the neighbors will here you. Yes, I want a warm up. Hey, Billy, bring Grampa his slippers, will you?" Grampa finally called back from the living room.

"He's already gone fishing with Ron," Nana said as she poured the coffee into the cup he was holding.

Grampa scowled and put his socks back on. In less than a minute, Nana came scurrying with his slippers. When she tried to help him put them on, he yanked them out her hands and put them on himself – with a lot of sighing and huffing and puffing, like he always did when things didn't go just exactly his way.

Sunrise At Two Lions

Chapter Two – Billy's Gone

Rachael's family owned a camp on Tacoma Lake that had been in the family for three generations. Ron had always loved going out there to fish and just relax, since before he graduated from high school. So, even though their marriage hadn't worked out, and Rachael's father didn't like Ron one bit, Nana gave Ron a key and told him take Billy to the camp whenever Billy wanted to go out there to fish or swim.

Ron parked at the top of the hill leading to the camp, so they wouldn't get stuck at the bottom of the hill on the snow and ice. They carried their backpacks, fishing gear and cooler down the hill past the cabin to the lake while Ron's Irish setter, Queenie, jumped and barked and ran around them as they made their way. Queenie loved coming out to the lake, where she could run free through the woods. She was too hyper for Billy's liking.

They walked over to where the big pine trees, maples and white birches hung out over the lake. In the summer, the water was usually a lot cooler in this spot because the thick grouping of trees blocked the sun from ever hitting that part of the lake directly. It was a great spot to cool off on a hot summer day. And they go could go over just a few yards to the clearing when they wanted to sunbathe and enjoy warmer water.

Ron cut a few branches from a low-hanging pine tree and put

most of their stuff on top of the branches to keep it off the snow-covered ground. Then he rubbed his gloved hands together and said to Billy, "Let's do it."

Ron reached out and put his hand on Billy's chest and stopped him just before they stepped out on the ice. There had been a January thaw for the past few days and even though they were in the shaded area, Ron wanted to be sure the ice was safe. So he walked out a few steps, then jumped up and down hard a few times. He thought he heard a crack, but tried several times more and didn't hear it again, so he motioned Billy to come on out.

It was almost noon before the flags were finally all set. Billy and Ron had set out about a dozen flags. If you're not familiar with ice fishing, it's done by chopping a round hole about a foot or so in diameter, in the ice, which by the time it's safe to walk on, is nearly a foot thick. The chopping is done with a heavy iron bar with a chiseled end. It can take quite a bit of time and definitely requires concentration. Inattentive people have been known to chop off a toe or two.

Once the hole is cut, you just drop a line in and wait. People who fish are people who are very good at waiting. The fishing line is attached to a little red flag on a wooden stick, which is bent over in a half circle, and spring loaded. When a fish takes the hook, the pull releases the flag, which then pops up to let you know that a fish is on the line.

They had been out on the ice of Tacoma Lake for about two hours, chopping away at the ice, and Billy was down to his T-shirt because of the sweat he had worked up chopping holes in the ice. The sun was unusually warm this day, but his feet were freezing, and he was hungry. So, he was really glad to see his father open a thermos, pour a couple of cups of hot cocoa and unwrap two sandwiches.

Queenie, who had been running through the woods like she

always did when they came to the lake, immediately appeared, running and sliding on the ice. She came right over beside Billy, when she saw him take a bite of ham sandwich. Billy lifted his sandwich and turned away so Queenie wouldn't snatch it away from him.

"No, Queenie. Sit!" Billy tried, to no avail, as Queenie ran around him to get even closer to his sandwich. But when Ron spoke Queenie sat right down on her haunches and just licked her chops while Billy began to eat his sandwich.

"I'm not giving you any, Queenie!" Billy snapped.

Billy loved baked ham sandwiches. And he was picking around the edges, sipping on his cocoa, savoring every bite of his ham sandwich, until he could chomp into the delicious, thickest, tastiest bite in the middle.

"Hey, Billy, there goes one."

Billy set his cocoa down carefully on the top of the cooler, wrapped his sandwich quickly, set it down, too, and sprinted for the flag.

He was hoping for a nice big bass. A pickerel would be good, but they were kind of bony. A white perch would be edible, but definitely not his favorite. And if it were a yellow perch, which is just about all bones, he'd just throw it back. It was none of these. False alarm. The line was empty. Sometimes the pickerel would hit the line so hard they would snap it.

"Dammit!" Billy sputtered, then looked around quickly to make sure his father hadn't heard him. As it turned out, Billy looked just in time to see Queenie make off with the best part of his sandwich.

"Dammit, Queenie!"

Ron just smiled and shook his head in mock disgust. Then he burst out laughing. That made Billy laugh, too. Maybe it was the cold and the fact that they were very tired, or maybe because of Billy's relief that he didn't get in trouble for saying what he said, but anyway, they were both soon rolling around on the ice laughing and holding onto their stomach like, as Grampa often said, "a couple of damn fools."

Three pickerel, no bass, and about two dozen white perch later, they packed it in. It was starting to get dark and they had quite a long way to walk to get back up the hill where they had parked the Jeep.

When they made it to the top of the rise, they saw a very faint beam from the Jeep headlights. Ron had forgotten to turn the lights off and, sure enough, the battery was deader than a mackerel.

Since there was no electricity or phone at the camp, and this was before cell phones, they had no choice. They had to stay in the cabin for the night and go for help in the morning. So they cooked some of the day's catch over the fireplace and drank the rest of the cocoa. Ron found plenty of blankets and they wrapped up, snuggled together next to the fireplace, and went to sleep.

A few hours later, Billy had to go to the bathroom so badly, he had no choice but to brave the pitch-black of night and trudge through the snow to the outhouse. When he came out, he somehow got turned around and headed off away from camp. He didn't realize it until he came to a flat clearing. Then he knew he had gone the wrong way. He thought he was at the open edge of the lake. But he wasn't. He was several feet out on it.

He heard the ice crack and somehow he knew it was too late to do anything about it. He stood absolutely still on the spot and inhaled a quick gulp of air. Then, like a shot, he dropped through the ice. With his lungs full of air, he quickly bobbed back up. But he hit thicker ice, face up, farther out into the lake.

He punched at the ice above and held his breath as long as he could. He used to practice holding his breath in the swimming pool back at Nana's and he was really good at it. But sooner or later he had to let it go. When he finally did, though, his breath didn't go anywhere. Billy was face up under the ice; eyes shut tight, cheeks puffed way out – frozen solid.

During the night a light snowfall covered Billy's tracks and his whereabouts. When Ron woke up at about 7 am, he looked for Billy somewhere in the pile of blankets. No Billy. When he didn't find him anywhere in the cabin, he went outside to look for him. Ron thought he probably was getting something out of the Jeep or he was in the outhouse. But by now it was snowing hard and you couldn't see more than a few feet in front of you.

"Billy!" Ron shouted several times. Then he checked the Jeep and the outhouse. No Billy. For a while, Ron wasn't worried at all. He figured Billy was checking something in the woods and Queenie would find him in no time. But Queenie came back from her romp alone, and after about a half-hour, Ron became concerned. He walked to the top of the hill, shouted Billy's name over and over for about another ten minutes, and then started to walk around the lake. Still no Billy. Ron was beginning to get very worried, and a little frantic.

He decided to walk out to the road and hitchhike into Gardiner for a phone, and for someone to help him start his Jeep. He thought, or at least hoped, that Billy would be safely back in the cabin by the time he got back.

The first car to come by didn't see Ron through the snow-storm until they got really close. They swerved away and just beeped the horn, waved, and kept on going. The second vehicle to come by was a police cruiser, and it stopped.

In less than an hour, about 30 or 40 people were walking the woods and edge of the lake looking for Billy. A couple of them started to go out on the ice to get a better look into a section of the woods, but scurried off the ice when they heard it crack once or twice. For some strange reason, it never occurred to them what had happened to Billy.

Days went by; weeks went by, still no Billy. There was a gloom and sadness that hung in the air after Billy's disappearance that the families couldn't shake. Even the normally boisterous and rowdy Fraser family couldn't let it go. Ron's mother openly took it really hard. Nana's stoic French Canadian upbringing prevented her from showing too much emotion, but she missed Billy terribly.

The local and statewide news ran stories of Billy's disappearance almost every day for about a month. The second month, the stories died down, and by the third month, Billy was given up for dead by just about everybody but Nana.

She insisted that something in her bones told her Billy was alive and he would be back. And she refused to go to a memorial service that Ron's mother asked the family to hold. It was just a quiet family affair, really sad, and Ron's mother was the only one who could stop crying long enough to even say a few words. After that, life went back to it's usual routine, except for the black cloud that hung in the air. All of that was about to change.

Exactly 90 days from that fateful ice-fishing trip, on a bright and sunny April day in Maine, as the noonday sun beat down on Tacoma Lake, an extraordinary event took place. Billy's tightly closed eyes and puffed out cheeks were just below the surface of the wafer-thin ice. Everything was still and quiet, except for a few early robins' chirping. Then, in a startling instant, Billy's eyes sprung open wide and a fierce exhale burst out through the thin ice.

By some miracle of hibernation, or cryogenics, or some such thing, Billy was alive. As soon as his breath let go, he came thrashing up and out of the water, crashing through the surface and splashing his way until he was up on the grass and pine needles at the edge of the lake.

"Dad!" he started shouting over and over, as if what happened to him had just happened a few minutes ago. He got up, ran to the cabin, and pushed open the door before reality hit him. He spun around to see bare ground outside. It wasn't winter anymore. Dad and Queenie, and the Jeep, were gone.

He thought he was going to faint, but a cold chill running right down to his bones snapped him out of it. He took off his wet clothes, wrapped himself up in one of the blankets on the floor and looked for some paper to start the fireplace.

In just a few minutes the fireplace was blazing and Billy was beginning to feel the shivers that kept coming every few seconds slow down. His mind had been so much on getting the fire going and getting warm that he hadn't had time to think. But as he slowly warmed up, he began to get flashes of what seemed like a dream.

As his mind tried to reconcile what was happening, he was distracted again. This time by hunger pangs. He found canned beans and some cold cereal left over from last summer. He ate the beans cold and the stale cereal dry. Then he fell asleep.

When he woke up, the fireplace was down to smoldering ashes and his clothes were just about dry. His boots were still pretty wet, so he lit the stove and tucked them in the gas oven, and then hung his pants over the door of the oven. He checked on his boots every few minutes, and when they were dry, slipped his still chilled feet into his toasty-warm boots.

He was still really confused, still shivering every so often and still really hungry. Now he wanted desperately to go home. So he made his way out to the edge of the road and started walking.

It was very quiet along the road, no traffic at all. The warm afternoon sun felt nice on his back and the quiet gave him time to think. His mind flashed to a picture of a mansion or a castle at the end of a long driveway. He heard the sounds of ocean waves crashing on the shore and soft classical music. None of it made any sense to him.

He hadn't walked more than several hundred yards before he realized how incredibly weak he felt. He stopped walking and leaned against a fence that enclosed a rolling pasture on the side of the road. He felt dizzy and tried to shake it off, but stumbled and fell on the gravel at the edge of the paved road. The next thing he heard was the sound of a car stopping, and a car door opening and closing.

"Young man, are you all right?" someone excitedly repeated several times before he could respond. Looking up he saw a woman who looked like one of his old schoolteachers leaning over him. "I saw you take a fall just as I was coming by. Do you need a ride home?" Then she repeated, "Are you all right?"

No sooner were the words out of her mouth than she recognized Billy. She gasped, mouth open, and seemed to go into a freeze frame for what seemed like a full minute to Billy. She looked like she had seen a ghost, was all he could think.

"Billy! Billy! My God, you're Billy Fraser. Is that really you, Billy?"

"Can you give me a ride to Nana's?" Billy asked sheepishly. He wasn't sure what all the fuss was about. He had just stumbled, that's all. "Yeah, I'm OK."

Mrs. Littlefield, who had been Billy's fourth grade teacher, kept looking over at Billy, but only said, "My God," over and over as they drove to Billy's house. When they pulled in the driveway, Billy jumped out of the car and ran in through the kitchen door.

Chapter Three – Billy's Home

As Billy came into the kitchen, Nana was leaning over taking an apple pie out of the oven. Now, you remember Nana had a high-pitched voice. Well, she had high-pitched emotions and energy to go along with her voice.

"Hi, Nan. I'm starving," were the first words out of Billy's mouth, like he had just come in from playing outside for a while.

Nana jumped at the sound of his voice, but managed to hold onto the hot apple pie she was taking out of the oven. As she looked up with a disgusted scowl on her face, to see who had, "scared her out of her wits", as she liked to say, her expression changed from scowling to horrified. She was sure she was seeing a ghost.

This time she didn't hold onto the pie, she startled so violently that she flipped the pie in Billy's direction. It smacked on the floor and slid to a stop at his feet.

He was so famished and disoriented that he didn't stop to think. He scooped up some of the piping hot pie and stuffed it into his mouth. Just as the burning sensation hit his tongue and throat, he felt the sting of a ferocious slap to his face. A deafening, blood-curdling screech of his name immediately followed that. It was all too much. Billy passed out.

"Billy! Billy! Billy!" Nana screamed and cried. The whole

unbelievable scene made her feel like she was really going out of her wits this time. If Mrs. Littlefield hadn't come through the door the next second, Nana might have really lost her mind.

"I saw him walking out near Tacoma Lake. I didn't know who he was at first. He stumbled and fell on the side of the road, so I stopped to see if he was all right. Is he all right? I can't believe it's really Billy." And once more, "Is he all right?"

Nana looked up with a crazed expression. She was tightly gripping handfuls of hair on the top of her head with both hands and it looked like she could pull out clumps of hair any second. She looked like she had gone absolutely insane. The sound of Mrs. Littlefield's voice is probably the only thing that kept her from completely losing it. She was making grunting and snarling sounds and holding her teeth clinched together.

Mrs. Littlefield knelt down beside her and put her arm around her to try to calm her down. The sounds Nana was making were getting louder and more hysterical until Billy opened his eyes for just a second, said, "I'm sorry, Nana," and closed them again. Nana snapped out of it, shook him, and he opened his eyes again. He had a dazed expression, but managed a faint smile.

"Oh, Billy. I didn't mean to hit you. You scared the wits out of me. Where have you been? What happened to you? What..."

"Nana, can I have some water? My mouth hurts a lot," Billy pleaded.

Mrs. Littlefield asked if she should call Dr. Matthews. Nana thought for a minute. She hated to call on doctors. She was an herbalist of sorts and had great faith in the body's ability to heal itself. This time she relented and asked Mrs. Littlefield if she would call and see when the doctor could come over.

After Mrs. Littlefield convinced Dr. Matthews that it really was Billy and, no, they couldn't bring him to his office or the hospital, he was in bed, exhausted, Dr. Matthews agreed to come over. He said he be there at the end of the day, around 5:30.

Nana called Ron, then Ron's mother, and finally she placed a long-distance call to Rachael in Florida. Ron's mother came in from across the street first and cried and cried at the site of Billy. He was sitting up, and smiled a weak smile without a word. When she hugged him, he patted her gently on the back and said softly, "I'm OK, Grammie, I'm OK."

"Where have you been, Billy? What happened to you?" Ron's mother asked. But Billy just looked kind of dazed and confused by the question. It took him a long time to answer, but finally he spoke.

"I fell through the ice."

Ron came crashing through the front door, almost ripping it off the hinges, and running through the kitchen. He saw Nana and Mrs. Littlefield looking into the downstairs bedroom, off the kitchen, and slowed down just enough not to knock them down.

When he looked in and saw Billy sitting on the bed, Ron hesitated for a brief moment and then, in one leap, landed on the bed. This bounced Billy up and into Ron's arms. Ron held on tightly and kept rubbing the back of Billy's head.

"Thank you, God. Oh, thank you, God." Ron cried over and over. His mother and Nana looked at each other with a subdued smile. They were both churchgoers, but Ron had never really wanted anything to do with it and hadn't been to church since he was a kid. The tears started. The crying started. Then the relieved laughter started.

Soon Nana and Ron and Ron's mother were all hugging and rocking Billy at the same time. Mrs. Littlefield looked a little uneasy for few seconds, but then joined in the group hug, all of them laughing and crying.

"What's going on here?" a voice boomed. Billy's grandfather had come home.

Nana looked up first. "It's Billy. Billy's home. He's OK. Dr. Matthew's is coming over."

Billy's grandfather didn't acknowledge what Nana had said. He glared at Ron and said, "You had him all the time, didn't you? You..."

Nana's high pitch reached a new level. "You shut up! You just shut up! Shut up. Shut up. Shut up."

Now that stunned everybody, probably including Nana. She never confronted Billy's grandfather. But this time she was worried more about Billy than his grandfather. And she let him have it.

His face went its usual beet red, warning-light color, to signal the coming explosion. But he didn't say a word back. He turned and walked out, slamming the door behind him, and chirping the tires like an angry teenager as he drove away.

Dr. Matthews turned in the driveway about this time, glanced back at the car roaring down Winter Hill, got out of his car and walked into the house. Nana heard the door and readied herself for the coming barrage she expected. When she saw it was Dr. Matthews, she breathed a sigh of relief and grabbed the doctor's sleeve to pull him into Billy's room.

"He seems fine. Everything's normal. A little skinny, but other than that, he's healthy," was the good doctor's pronouncement. "The only problem is, he has absolutely no recall of the past 90 days, except for falling through the ice on the lake.

"His memory should come back, though, and it could come back anytime, either gradually over time or in a sudden flash. But it most probably will come back. Of course, a traumatic event can some-times wipe out the memory completely. We'll just have to wait and see. If you like, I'll have him taken in to the hospital for a few tests, just to be sure that there's no brain damage or internal injury, but he seems to be just fine."

Nana abruptly refused the hospital tests option and put on water for tea. Mrs. Littlefield and Dr. Matthews agreed to have some tea with Nana while Ron stayed to talk with Billy. Ron's mother remembered that she had left something on the stove and quickly zipped out the door, saying she would be back in a few minutes. While she waited for the water to heat up, Nana started mixing up pancakes for Billy.

"So what happened to you? We were going nuts."

"I fell through the ice and that's all I remember. I made it to shore and you were gone."

"When did you fall through the ice?"

"When I got up to go to the outhouse. When we stayed at camp. It was really dark. I got turned around, I guess. When the Jeep wouldn't start, last night. You know."

Ron paled. He told Billy that they had gone ice fishing in January. It was back then that the Jeep wouldn't start, because he had left the lights on. But that was three months ago. It was three months ago, not last night.

"It's April, Billy. You've been gone for three months. We thought you had been kidnapped or killed or something. We've been going crazy. Where were you for three months?"

Billy just stared blankly and then started to cry. He couldn't remember anything except falling through the ice and holding his breath for as long as he could.

"I tried to find you, Dad. I looked everywhere, but you were gone. I was soaking wet and I had to dry my clothes. I fell asleep and when I woke up I started walking."

"It's OK, Billy. It's OK. We're just glad you're home."

"Can I get something to eat?" Billy asked. "I'm starved."

No sooner had Billy spoken the words than Nana appeared carrying a breakfast tray with a stack of pancakes on it. Also on the tray was a cup of maple syrup that she had warmed up in the oven for a minute – just the way Billy liked it, and a tall glass of cold milk.

After Dr. Matthews and Mrs. Littlefield left, Nana poured herself another cup of tea and pulled a kitchen chair up beside Billy's bed. Ron was still sitting on the bed, just smiling and watching Billy wolf down his pancakes. Every so often, Ron would shake his head slightly and quickly wipe away the first sign of a tear.

"Did you call Rachael?" he asked Nana.

"Of course, Ron. She's on her way from Florida."

"Mom's coming home?" Billy squeaked.

Nana popped her eyes wide open and shook her head "yes".

"Oh, look Billy!" Nana said loudly, pointing into her empty teacup. "You've been on a long journey. And there's a little dog trailing you."

Nana was not only an herbalist; one of the talents for which she was most well known was that she "read" tealeaves. It was a long-standing topic of conversation and jokes among all of her family and friends. And, of course, Grampa would never have anything to do with any of it.

But rarely did anyone in the family or circle of friends visit without a request for a reading. And Nana was always willing to accommodate. It was one of those things that you pretend to mock, but you're all ears when it's about you.

"Let me see, Nana."

Billy looked into the usual nondescript (except to Nana) scattering of the tealeaves at the bottom of the teacup. Nana pointed at a section and went on with the story of what see saw.

She saw this long winding road, a young man carrying a sack over his shoulder and a little dog jumping up near the young man. In the distance she saw a castle.

"See." She kept saying, as she told the story.

"A young man is on this long and winding road. A little dog is his companion, and they are approaching a castle. Now, a castle is a very powerful and magical symbol. It stands for strength and authority and wisdom. And it is very well protected, so that nothing can come against it.

"The little dog, jumping and barking, represents those thoughts we have when we are not sure about something, or when something is nagging at us, like things we wish we hadn't done, or when we are afraid of something that is about to happen."

Nana looked up from her reading. Billy had stopped chewing his pancakes and was staring off into space with his mouth still full. He sat motionless as he listened to Nana's reading.

"Did you remember something, Billy?" Nana asked, noticing his stillness.

"Uh? Oh, no, I was just listening, Nana. But I could hear some really soft music while you were talking. Weird."

"Hello," came Ron's mother's voice as she walked into the kitchen. "How's my Billy?"

"I'm fine, Grammie."

She peeked in to see him and said that she would be back after dinner to visit with him if that was all right.

Later in the evening, Billy moved to the living room couch, still wrapped up in a couple of blankets. He spent the evening watching television. Nana brought in snacks for him and Ron every so often. And Ron sat at Billy's feet, rubbing them to keep them warm, and to make physical contact with the son he thought he had lost forever.

Billy and Ron fell asleep on the couch. When Nana saw them, she didn't have the heart to wake them up. They looked so peaceful and happy. It was the first time that Nana noticed how much Billy looked like Ron.

The following day, Nana was in the kitchen, cooking dinner. Ron and Billy had hardly moved all day. Nana brought them breakfast and lunch in the living room. Other than that she pretty much left them alone to rest and recuperate.

At 5:00 p.m. on the dot, Grampa came through the door. He had stayed out all night and the whole day. He glared at Nana standing over the stove, his cold expression daring her to say something. She didn't. She just pointed at the table, already set for dinner.

"It's almost ready. Sit down."

Grampa stood where he was, to make the point that he wasn't about to jump just because she spoke. Nana caught his lingering expression, and thought to herself that she certainly knew where Rachael got that imperious look.

The kitchen door forcefully swinging open and smacking Grampa on the backside interrupted his studied, I'm-still-mad look. Grampa was no longer center stage. Rachael was home.

"Billy!" she screamed.

Grampa had bent forward and grabbed the kitchen table to keep his balance after the door hit him, so his left ear was right at the height of Rachael's mouth when she screamed. Grampa's instinctive reaction to lift his hand to protect his ear was enough to throw him off balance. He tumbled onto the edge of the table, flipping it up and knocking everything off, as he crashed to the floor in the midst of broken dishes and spilled food.

Billy came running out of the living room to greet his mother. Ron came right behind him. The three of them hugged tightly and stood locked together, rocking each other, crying. Nana watched with an adoring look, tears welling up in her eyes.

Grampa sat on the floor, stunned for a minute, and then he did something completely unexpected for a grouch. He broke into uproarious laughter. That stunned everyone else. Rachael, Ron, Billy and Nana all turned to look at Grampa sitting on the floor, in a mess. He had mashed potato in his hair, a piece of a broken serving dish delicately balancing on the top of his head, and a huge gravy stain making its way down the shoulder of his crisply starched white shirt.

Talk about comic relief. Nana fell against the kitchen wall, laughing so hard that she started coughing and choking, as she did a slow motion slide down to her knees on the floor.

Ron was beside himself laughing, but managed to compose himself enough to help Grampa up off the floor. Billy was slapping himself on his thigh so hard it stung.

Rachael kept asking Grampa if he was OK, and even though she tried to sound seriously concerned, her words were broken up by spurts of laughter.

"OK, that's it. We're all going out to dinner to celebrate. I'm buying." Rachael announced with a determined finality. "Let's go."

Ron said they couldn't go with the kitchen in such turmoil, but Nana said to just leave it. Grampa smiled and said he needed just a minute to wash up and change his shirt.

Billy watched all this going on with his mouth wide open. His mother and father together, his father in Billy's grandfather's house, his grandfather actually laughing and smiling, Nana leaving a mess in the kitchen; this was not normal. Maybe something strange really had happened to him.

It only took Grampa a minute to clean up and as soon as he was ready, they all started to go out the front door. Ron opened the door and stopped in his tracks. The media had made it to Gardiner. News travels fast in a small town.

Flash bulbs were going off, microphones were held up high, hoping to grab a sound bite, and two TV cameras from Portland stations were poised just off the front steps.

Billy poked his head through the grown-ups to get a better look. When he did, a flashbulb popped just a couple of feet from his eyes. And suddenly, it all came flooding back. Billy remembered, just like Dr. Matthews had said could happen, in a flash.

Rachael spoke up for the family and explained that they were all just going out to dinner to enjoy some family time together, and how they would all be glad to answer any questions and do interviews tomorrow, but not right now. Of course, that didn't stop the reporters from firing off questions, and it didn't stop photographers from firing off flashbulbs.

"Tomorrow." Rachael told them all. That's all she said. The rest of the family, including Billy, just pointed to Rachael when reporters turned to them, and no one else said a word.

Of course, a few of the reporters and photographers followed them to the restaurant. But when they saw it wasn't going to do any good, they left the family alone. Several of them handed Rachael their business cards and pressed for interview times. All they heard in response was, "tomorrow, tomorrow, tomorrow".

Billy was pretty quiet through dinner and dessert. During dinner, Nana caught him looking at his mother with the softest eyes and most pleasant smile she had ever seen on his face. On the way home, Billy announced matter-of-factly, "I remember what happened."

Chapter Four – Billy's Story

So, as soon as they came in, they all gathered in the living room. Billy sat on the couch. Ron sat beside him. Nana and Rachael sat on the floor by Billy's feet. Grampa sat in his chair. And Billy began to tell this story:

Just as I fell through the ice, I took a big gulp of air and shut my eyes and my mouth really tight. I don't remember the water even being cold. I sank pretty fast and then I came back up, but I hit the ice and couldn't find the hole I fell through. I tried to break the ice above me by hitting it, but I couldn't punch very hard through the water. I held my breath as long as I could and when I finally let it go, it didn't go anywhere.

Everything was quiet and dark for a little while, and then I saw this beautiful blue cloud, with streaks of light coming up behind it. It was the most beautiful blue I had ever seen.

Then the cloud disappeared and all I could see was checkered light. It was like a bunch of icicles in circles that got bigger and bigger. And the light was reflecting off them and the light was bouncing and sparkling all over the place. It looked like checkered light. That was all I could think.

This went on for a long time, until the checkered light stopped and everything turned black again, but only for a second.

Then I saw lightening bolts flashing and I heard the sound of a musical train. The sound was like a flute, but it was chugging like the rhythm of a train on the tracks, ka-chug, ka-chug, ka-chug, ka-chug. It was a happy sound and I forgot about the lightening bolts and just listened.

When the music stopped, I noticed that I had this really funny, nice taste in my mouth. It was kind of like honey, but more like a fruit juice. I could taste it like I was drinking it, but I wasn't drinking anything. It was like it was coming from inside of me, and I could taste it everywhere. I mean all inside my body. It was like I could feel it and taste it from my toes up to the tip of my tongue. It was sweet and delicious. It made me want to start laughing.

The lightening came back after a while, but this time it was green and red, and round. It flashed like lightening, but it looked like big round bulbs, full of light, on a Christmas tree. The lights came and went over and over for a long time.

Then I saw this man. Well, I think it was a man. Anyway, it looked like he was glowing. It was like I was on this mountain and I could see big rocks and trees and a trail. The man was standing just off the trail. I was kind of floating, kind of walking, toward him.

When I got really close, he turned his head and looked along the trail. He didn't say anything to me, but I knew he wanted me to look down the trail, too. When I did, I saw a big light that was shaped like a great big egg. It was about fifty feet away from me.

The next thing I knew, I was inside this big, egg-shaped light and I was floating in it. That's when God came.

"OK, that's enough for me." Grampa said, as he jumped up and headed for his bedroom without another word, leaving the rest of the family in the living room.

"I'm really tired, too, Billy." Rachael followed, as she stood up. Then she motioned for Ron to come with her into the kitchen.

Nana didn't move a muscle. That is, until she heard Rachael call her from the kitchen. When Nana went into the kitchen, Rachael was standing there wide-eyed. Ron put his hands up in an, "I'm helpless," gesture.

"Ma, we can't let Billy talk to anybody else about this," Rachael started. "They'll want him to undergo psychiatric treatment. The press will make us look like a bunch of lunatics. I can't go on television. I'm not talking to them, or anyone, about this. And Billy's not going to talk to them either. Did you hear what he said? He said, 'That's when God came.'"

Nana didn't respond to Rachael. She frowned, turned around, and headed back into the living room. She found Billy fast asleep. He had a peaceful, beautiful smile on his face. So, Nana carried him up to his room and tucked him in.

Rachael carried on most of the night, drinking coffee and pacing the kitchen floor, repeating over and over, "We can't let Bill talk about this." Ron was kind of worried that she was losing it, but he was more concerned with Billy. Nana just let Rachael babble on, knowing that things would take their course. Nana sure wanted to hear more about what happened to Billy. She was fascinated, and couldn't wait to hear more of Billy's story.

Nana finally asked Rachael what she was so upset about, and why she was so adamant about Billy not talking. Rachael had her reasons, but she didn't know how to talk to her mother about them, or she didn't want to.

Out of sheer exhaustion, Rachael finally wound down and went to bed. Ron slept on the couch. Nana went up and tucked Billy in one more time, and gave him a gentle kiss on the forehead. She was just happy that her Billy was home, safe and sound. Rachael wasn't too sure about the sound part. And Nana wasn't too sure about Rachael. Billy and Nana slept well that night.

The next words heard in the house were, "Billy, get up, your breakfast is getting cold."

When Billy came down to breakfast, Nana wasn't in her usual kitchen spot. Billy had never seen Nana sit at the kitchen table except to eat a meal, and then only after everyone else was seated. She was usually at the sink or at the stove. But this morning she was sitting down at the table, a cup of tea in front of her.

Billy's breakfast was right where it always was, in the perfect order, just the way he liked it.

Grampa had already left for work. Ron got up and left when he heard Grampa in the kitchen, and Rachael was still sleeping.

"So, what happened when God came?" Nana asked as Billy took his last sip of juice. Billy picked up right where he had left off the night before:

It's really hard to put into words, Nana. I couldn't see God, I just knew that God was there with me. I just felt so loved. It was like I was being held like a baby.

I was floating in this big cloud of light. It was like I was in a dream, but it was so real. God didn't speak, but I knew that everything was OK about everything. I was just so happy. I could feel so much love, and like God knew just who I was, and I knew that God was going to always be with me. It was like God was right inside me, Nana, or I was right inside God. It was like I knew everything was always going to work out OK in my life, like God had a plan for me, for my whole life. It's all about trust. Trusting this God of Love.

I knew in a weird way, almost like how everything works in

life. I don't mean like how the TV works and stuff like that, but how everything fits into place like it's supposed to fit.

I could feel that it's all perfect. Everything in life is perfect. Even when it seems really bad, its still perfect in a way we don't understand. When we see the way God sees it, it's like there are no questions about anything anymore.

Everything is answered if we just listen, and trust that everything is OK. We don't have to worry. God will take care of us, if we let him. God has this incredible love for everyone of us. God loves everyone, Nana. We can know that in our heart. I know that in my heart. God's love is so sweet.

Anyway, the next thing I knew, it was like I was walking on a road. Well, it wasn't a road it was more like a really long driveway. And I could see this really, really big house. It was like a castle, and it almost looked like it was shining because you could see the ocean behind it, only about a hundred yards away. Everything was shining. The trees, and rocks, and the grass were so shiny and beautiful.

I even stopped and sat down, because I wanted to look closer at a blade of grass, and it was so awesome. I could see these little tiny stripes in it. And the way it was divided in half by this perfect groove. All I could think was that God just made the grass so beautiful, so perfect. And there was this little purple flower with yellow and white, and a little black dot in the center. And…

"So what about the castle?" Nana asked. She didn't want to interrupt the story, but she couldn't contain herself anymore. She was really excited. The tealeaves' reading she had done for Billy the day before popped into her mind while Billy was telling his story. But before Billy could answer, someone else spoke.

"So what's for breakfast?" Rachael managed to get out through a big yawn and stretch.

Nana jumped up automatically to accommodate Rachael, just like she did for everyone. Billy was looking straight ahead out of the window over the kitchen sink. It was like he didn't even see his mother, and it looked like he had gone into a trance. But it was just that he was remembering every detail of what had happened to him so clearly, as he told Nana about it.

Then he almost shouted to Nana, who was just around the corner taking bacon and eggs out of the refrigerator, that he had to tell her about the lions.

"Um, Billy, I need to talk to you," Rachael said quite seriously. "Just finish your breakfast, OK. I got to have a coffee and then we'll talk."

"What about the lions?" Nana responded as she put the bacon and eggs on the kitchen counter.

"Ma," Rachael interrupted, a little too loudly, "can it wait? Billy and I need to talk."

So, Billy went back to eating his breakfast and Nana started cooking another breakfast for Rachael. Nana didn't drink coffee, but she always made some for Grampa, and there was some still in the coffee pot. Rachael poured herself a cup, and sat down at the kitchen table.

"You doing a garden this year, Ma?" she asked.

"Of course, I've got seedlings all ready to go. I'm going to plant a few more herbs this year."

"Still going to can mustard pickles and tomatoes?"

"Nope, no tomato canning. I read that cooked tomatoes aren't good for you. You should only eat them uncooked."

Rachael made sure to keep Nana involved in talk about her garden while Billy finished his breakfast. Then she asked Billy to come into the living room. Nana knew enough to leave them along to talk. She'd have plenty of time with Billy later.

Nana and Rachael were pretty classic mother and daughter opposites. Nana was a Momma Bear. She protected her children and her den, fiercely. She cooked and cleaned, and "kept house". That was her role as she saw it. In addition to that she kept close tabs on finances, making sure bills were paid on time. And that judiciousness spilled over into areas of life, as well. She liked life neat and orderly, and predictable. She didn't like surprises.

She seriously considered herself something of a psychic, able to predict, or know somehow, what was going to happen. So she wasn't "supposed" to be surprised by anything. And to make sure, she kept her life very orderly and organized.

Now, Rachael, on the other hand, was a spontaneous free spirit. Her room was always, always in chaos. It would have frightened a pack rat. But she stepped over the piles, and out of her room, looking like a princess; careful to shut the door behind her, so no one would see. No one would have guessed what turmoil went on inside of her room, and inside of her head.

She left her marriage, and she left her son. She didn't do it carelessly or maliciously. She was just a restless free spirit, looking for something. She wasn't sure what she was looking for, but she was sure she hadn't found it. Part of her was convinced that she never would.

She often felt like she was being punished for something that she had done when she was younger. It was her "big secret", like so many of us have, and she never shared it with anyone. She just put on this devil-may-care front, coming and going as she pleased.

Whenever she popped in, announced, unannounced, or whatever, she acted like she expected everyone to be delighted to see her. Whatever the circumstances had been of her last departure, to her that was history, and had no relevance to her new adventure. And the truth was, because she was so gorgeous and sparkly, everyone was delighted to she her, and usually eager to hear of her latest adventure.

So Nana and Rachael had a few things to work out as Rachael grew up and matured. Well, the maturity part was always a pretty big question in Nana's mind. Rachael rebelled at any attempt to control, very early. And she outlasted Nana on every issue, from picking up her room, or rather not picking up her room, to what she wore and how she swore. She came into the world defiant and ready to stand her ground. She got that from her father.

When Rachael first left Billy with Nana for several months, and returned home, Nana tried to protect Billy from her, using Rachael's absence as an excuse for Nana to assert her role as surrogate parent over Rachael. That took one encounter to get straightened out permanently.

"You can't expect to come back here after being gone for four months, and just take right over again. Billy has been with me all this time, and I'm more like a mother to him." Nana started. That was as far as she got with that one. For all their differences, Rachael had a bit of Momma Bear in her as well. She blasted Nana with both barrels, threatening to take Billy with her, and never come back. Nana quickly called for a truce.

She backed off then, and she would back off now. She let them go in the living room by themselves, handing Rachael her bacon and eggs as they left. Nana had given up on trying to get Rachael to eat at the table like everyone else. That was another small battle that Nana lost, too. She started cleaning up the kitchen, and tried not to make too much noise, so she could hear what Billy and Rachael were talking about.

"Billy, you have to promise me that you will not tell anyone else about what happened to you, or even mention — I mean especially not mention what you said last night," Rachael started.

"You mean about God showing up?"

Rachael looked around the room like she actually thought the place could be bugged already. She shook her head yes, and then she shook her head no in disbelief. Billy was confused.

"No?" He asked.

"Yes, that!" Rachael sighed.

"Mom," Billy spoke very softly, almost as if he were speaking to a child. "It's OK. Everything is OK. It's OK that God showed up." Billy's soft response and the fact that he had a strangely calm, almost patronizing smile startled Rachael.

"Billy, God did not show up. Don't say that. People will think we're crazy if you say that. Come on, Billy. This is a small town. My God, Billy, what happened to you?"

"God," was Billy's soft reply to her.

"Oh, I can't talk to you," Rachael said. She was so exasperated by this whole thing with Billy, and so afraid that everyone would think that the whole family had gone nuts, or worse, religious nuts.

Now, you would have thought that Rachael wouldn't care what other people thought, being a free spirit and all. But, as you heard before, she had a real turmoil going on. And she put up a front to protect herself. She had a fear of being found out as a phony; a princess with a messy room. And it went a lot deeper than that.

Rachael carried a lot of guilt inside, and she didn't want to have anything to do with God. To her, God was a watchdog who just waited for everyone to mess up before condemning them to hell. And she knew she had messed up her life really badly. At least that's what she thought.

She remembered the way her grandmother used to say, "On

second thought, sure, give me another glass of wine. I'm going to hell anyway."

The first time Rachael heard that, she was about six years old. She never forgot it. And when she heard about hell in Sunday School, she closed off a big piece of her heart, because she felt so badly for her grandmother.

When her grandmother died, Rachael was about thirteen. At the funeral, she told God that she hated him. And to her mind, that meant she was going to hell, too. From that point on, Rachael went from being a goodie-two-shoes to being a hell-raiser. Whenever her conscience would bother her, her grandmother's phrase about going to hell anyway would ring in. That was a big part of why she didn't want to hear about anything about God.

Now, not all of this was conscious to her, or right on her mind when she was talking to Billy. She just knew that she was terrified of the thought of her son being ridiculed. And Billy's casual and quiet demeanor about the whole thing frustrated her even more.

"Billy, please," was all she could say at this point.

"Well, why don't you talk to Nana," Billy started to say. But Rachael cut him off.

"I don't have to talk to Nana. I'm your mother. And I'm telling you…"

This time Billy cut her off. He stood up and gave her a hug. Then he told her that he didn't expect her to understand, but that he was "supposed" to tell his story. And he added that he had a lot more to tell.

"All right, you're own your own then," was how she responded to him at this point. She gave him a look that communicated her utter disapproval, but she had no more to say. He gave her a verbal shot back, but he did it with a smile to take the edge off of his rightly inherited defiant look.

"That's nothing new."

With that Rachael went cold. She never touched the breakfast Nana had cooked for her. She just walked to her room, packed her bags, called a cab, and when it arrived, walked out the door without another word to anyone.

Normally, at least up to now, Billy would have felt badly about the exchange with his mother. But this time he felt differently. He was just calm and peaceful inside.

Even when he saw Rachael get into the cab, he didn't react any differently. He just went out to the kitchen and told his grandmother that his mother left in a cab. Nana just shook her head and kept on stirring the spaghetti sauce she was cooking.

"So, do you want to hear any more of what happened?" Billy asked her.

Nana didn't say anything, but she stopped stirring, rinsed the big wooden spoon, and quickly dried her hands with her ever-present apron. Then she put on water for a cup of tea, and pulled a chair up to the kitchen table, across from Billy. He smiled at Nana and asked her where he had left off before they were so rudely interrupted.

"You said something about a castle, and then you said you were going to tell me about the lions," she reminded him. So, Billy continued with his story:

The big house that looked like a castle had two cement lions on the front steps, one on each side. They looked really mean and, when I first saw them, they scared me. But when I saw that they weren't real, I just smiled at them.

I was standing there smiling at the lions, and feeling kind of silly because these lions that weren't real lions scared me. But then one of them yawned and said, "Hi, Billy. How's it going."

I started laughing. I just broke up laughing, probably because it was so weird and definitely because I was scared again. Then I heard another voice say, "Don't let those lions scare you, Billy. They can't move off the steps and they won't bother you unless you stop to listen to them."

When I turned around I saw this man standing there. He was dressed in dark clothes, and he had long dark hair. But he had a really nice smile. I asked him how they knew my name was Billy, and he said that he was expecting me, and so was everyone else. I didn't know what he meant by that right then. He told me that his name was William.

I said, "That's my name, too. Everybody just calls me Billy."

By now I had forgotten all about falling through the ice, and the light and everything, and it just felt right to be here at this big castle, this big house. Somehow I knew I was supposed to be there. Or at least, I didn't think about it. William made me feel safe. It was like he was there to protect me or teach me something. Anyway, I felt really good. It was like I was in a different world. Well, I guess I was in a different world.

William put his arm around my shoulder and said, "Let's go inside. Everybody's waiting for you." I still didn't know what he meant, but I was feeling really good and happy, so I started up the front stairs with William.

As we went past the lions, the one on the other side of the steps winked at me and whispered, "See you later, Billy." I asked William if he heard that. He nodded his head and told me again not to pay any attention to the lions.

When we went inside, I could smell apple pie cooking. It smelled just like yours, Nana, and I thought for a minute that I was back home. But I wasn't. This house was big and bright, with really high ceilings. I could hear music coming from somewhere, like the music I heard earlier when I first fell through the ice. We went through a big kitchen and then into a room like a porch. The porch has big windows and I could see the ocean about a hundred yards away. It was beautiful.

When we stepped out onto the porch, I saw a bunch of people sitting around a big long table, and some others sitting on chairs, and a few more people on a long blue couch. There were eleven people there. They all said, "Hi, Billy," at the same time. I don't know why, but I started laughing again. I wasn't scared this time. It felt it was my birthday party or something.

William took me around to each person and introduced me. I'll tell you their names later, when I tell you the stories they each had for me. William told me that while I was with them, I was going to hear twelve stories, one from each of the people I was meeting, and one from him.

He told me that he was going to tell me about the two lions, and that he would remind me of this after each of the stories I was about to hear. But first, he said that he was going to show me my room, upstairs. I started asking him a whole bunch of questions, but he just said that I would see.

"You'll see, Billy, you'll see." That's all he would say each time I asked him a question. So I just stopped asking him anything for a while.

My room was a big white room, with a king-size bed. Two big windows looked out over the ocean, and I could see the white caps, and hear one after another crash up on the beach. I noticed that even small, small waves made a pretty big crash sound as they turned over and hit the beach.

I could see little islands out in the ocean, not far from shore. I could smell the ocean air, and I could see seagulls flying around close to shore. Sometimes a lot of them would gather. And if one came up from the ocean with food or anything in its beak, the others would all try to get it. They really made a racket. It was fun to watch and it made me laugh.

On the beach, the sand was really flat. I saw little birds with long skinny legs. And they would scurry really fast. Their legs just made a blur. They made me laugh, too. Everything just seemed to make me want to laugh. Everything made me happy.

When I looked around the room I saw lots of paintings on the walls. The colors were really bright and they looked like what I saw when I looked out over the ocean. Well, they sort of looked like the ocean. But there were lots of colors in them that I didn't see out on the water. I looked back and forth at the paintings and the ocean a few times.

I was looking out over the water, just watching and listening, when the smell of that apple pie I mentioned got really strong. I turned around and there was a young girl about my age standing there with a slice of pie and a big glass of milk. She said to me, "Nana sent this up to you."

That really surprised me. I thought she meant you. But I guess it was her Nana. Anyway, I ate the pie and drank the milk. It was delicious. I remember every bite of that sweet, warm apple pie. The crust was just like yours, Nana. The milk tasted like the taste in my mouth that I tasted when I first fell through the ice.

It seemed that everything that was happening kept reminding me of those few minutes after I fell through the ice, and all those wonderful feelings. Then I lay down on the big bed and I guess I went to sleep.

I must have slept really well, because the next thing I knew, William was shaking me to wake me up. After I got up and took a shower in the bathroom right next to my room, I went back to my room to get dressed and there were clean clothes all ironed and laid out on the bed.

As I was getting dressed, I looked out of the windows of my room. The sun was just coming up over the ocean, and the colors in the sky and on the water were like colors I had never seen. I snapped my head around to look at the paintings in my room again, and then back out at the sunrise. This time I saw a lot of the colors that were in the paintings on the walls. I finished getting dressed and went downstairs.

I found William, and Anna, that was the girl who brought me the pie, another woman, and an older man named Wolfgang sitting out on the porch eating breakfast.

Everybody said, "Hi, Billy, your breakfast is ready," at the same time. When I heard them say that, it was like, all of a sudden, I was supposed to be there, and I knew them, and they knew me. Don't ask me how I knew that. I just did. It didn't even occur to me to ask where I was or why I was there, or anything. It just seemed right. And I was feeling really happy to be there. So I sat right down.

The breakfast table was covered with a white tablecloth, and the table was loaded with pastries that were filled with bright lemon fillings, and deep red raspberry colored filling, blueberry fillings, and there was all kinds of fresh fruit all cut up, a big clear glass pitcher of orange juice, and another one filled with cranberry juice right beside it.

The colors from the morning sky came in through the big window and mixed with all the colors on the breakfast table. I could see the colors from the paintings in my room everywhere on the table.

I was happy and feeling safe, but then I got a little scared when I sat down and looked at my plate. I saw a reflection of one of the lions from the front steps, looking back at me from the white plate. He didn't say anything this time, but I felt scared again for a second. That feeling went away as soon as I put a lemon pastry on my plate. When I started to eat, everything tasted better than anything I ever tasted.

Nobody said hardly anything all though breakfast. They just smiled at each other and smiled at me. We all looked out at the sunrise and watched the changing colors of pink and peach and gold and blue in the morning sky and then looked at each other and just smiled. It was fun doing that. Anna giggled once.

As soon as we finished breakfast, William asked me to take a walk with him. We went out through the kitchen and onto the front steps. The lions were there in their usual places. I kind of expected them to do something or say something as we went by them and walked down the steps, but they didn't.

We walked into a forest of mostly pine trees and white birches. There weren't many trees. Everything was open and the sunlight came through the branches and leaves in streams of light all over the place. It felt magical. The ground was covered mostly with leaves and pines needles. We saw a few chipmunks and squirrels as we walked. Pretty soon we came to a patch of light green moss, with some of those little white flowers that you showed me.

"Queen Anne's Lace," Nana said softly, breaking the spell she had been under. She had been totally entranced by Billy's story. And she was as much entranced by the details of the story, as she was the way Billy was telling it.

The way he described his experiences; the colors, the sounds, the setting, the taste, all with this look of sheer delight on his face that she had never seen before, just stunned her. Billy was definitely changed by his experience – whatever had happened to him.

Billy smiled at her and nodded acknowledgement when she told him the name of the little white flowers. And went right back to his story:

So, anyway, William and I sat down on the moss and just enjoyed the warm sun. We didn't talk or anything for the longest time. It just felt so peaceful and nice. After a little while, I leaned back on the moss and stared up through the trees to the sky. And William began to tell me a story.

He told me that the two stone lions on the steps at the house were originally put there to protect the house and everyone who came into it, and scare away anyone or anything that would come near the house that could hurt anyone in any way. They were supposed to just scare away anyone who didn't belong there, but after a while things changed.

The lions would roar and scare anyone who came by, even the people who came to visit or who came to live at the house. After a few years, they even began to talk to people coming by them. And what was even stranger, one of them seemed to know everything about everybody's life – especially anything they did wrong. And the other knew how to really scare everyone.

It was like they knew everyone, and they knew every detail of their secret fears and doubts. And they were really mean about it.

William explained to me that we all have things in our lives that we wish we hadn't done or hadn't said, and that most everyone has some doubts at times about who they really are and what they are all about, and what their purpose is in life.

I told him that I bet just about everyone was scared of snakes and spiders, and the dark when they were kids. He said a lot of grown ups are still scared of snakes and spiders and the dark, and lots of other things. They try to act brave and like these things don't bother them. But they don't fool the lions. And they sure don't fool themselves.

I asked him why the lions scared everybody, when they were just supposed to protect the house and the people in it. William told me that the lions figured out that an effective way to protect someone is to make them afraid of doing things that are dangerous, or beyond their abilities. That way they will stay safe. It's not a good way, but it works.

So they started telling everybody who came by to watch out for this and watch out for that, and not to try something that would possibly hurt them. But pretty soon they were warning people coming by about every little thing that wasn't part of their daily routine.

And if they wouldn't listen, then the lions would remind them of a time they got hurt or did something bad, to try to keep them from doing anything new or making any mistakes.

William said the lions were like over-protective parents and teachers. They meant well at first, but then they started controlling so much that they got everybody afraid to try anything, and doubting their ability to do just about anything. Even worse, they made the people they were trying to protect feel really bad about themselves, inside.

I wondered how anybody ever dared to try anything new or get to feel better about themselves after making a lot of mistake or doing something really bad, if the lions wouldn't let them forget what they had done, and I asked William about that. He told me that I would have my answer if I would listen carefully.

"Did you ever worry about something and get all in a fret about it, and it never happened?" William asked me.

"Sure, lots of times," I said. "One time I broke a glass in the kitchen when I was getting some milk, and I heard Grampa yell when he heard it break."

I told him how I was worried that Grampa was going to get all upset and ground me and everything, but after all the fretting I did, this time Grampa just let it go without being upset at all.

And then I told about coming home late from school one time, and another time thinking I had failed a math test, and then about getting picked on and rescued before anything happened. I had a lot of stories about worrying and being scared of something happening that didn't happen the way I thought it would.

William just listened patiently, and then he told me something about the lions. He told me, once again, that the lions are not real. They can talk and all, but they can't really move or do anything directly. And they can only talk if we are around to listen to them, and if we stop and listen to them, they will talk and talk and talk.

I was wondering what this had to do with him worrying about stuff that never really happened, when William told me the names of the lions.

He told me that the lion on the left was Furman. He is the lion of fear. Furman likes to fret, and he's always worried about what's going to happen in the future, what happened in the past, and what other people think. He's always afraid. He's always worried. He thinks everything is going to go wrong, and he's always warning everybody about bad things that are going to happen all the time.

On the right, William went on, is Dunbar. Dunbar is the lion of doubt. He's a lot like Furman, except it's not so much fear as indecision that he talks about all the time. Should I do this? Should I do that? What if I do this? What if I do that? How will I feel if I do? How will I feel if I don't? How will I feel after I do, or after I don't? What do I want to do with my life?

And, he, too, worries a lot about what other people will think. He worries that they won't like him, or they'll think he's strange or different.

I just kind of laughed and told William that if these lions were just made of stone, and they couldn't do anything, what did we have to fear from them anyway? He told me we didn't have anything to fear. It's just that when we stop and listen to them, we listen to fear and doubt that they try to put in us and make us think about all the time.

William reminded me of how he had told me that the lions were originally there on the steps leading into the house to protect the people who lived in the house. But they got too big for britches and instead of just protecting the people from anything that would hurt them from the outside, they started to warn the people in the house about every little thing.

And then it just went on from there. They started talking and talking to everyone who went into the house, and causing worry and doubt about everything.

"Oh, yeah," I said. "I'm beginning to understand. So fear and doubt are supposed to protect us. But if we let them, they try to take over and make us worry about stuff we don't have to worry about, right?"

He told me that I was exactly right, but that there is a way to conquer the lions, and he would tell me. But it was getting late and we needed to go back to the house. He said he would tell me later. So we got up from the moss and headed back to the house. I couldn't believe it was getting dark. It seemed like we had just got there.

On the way back to the house, William asked me if I had seen the paintings in my room, and I told him that I had, and that I liked them, and I saw their colors everywhere, it seemed. He asked me if I had a favorite painting, but I didn't. Then he asked me if I would go to my room when we got back to the house, and pick any one of the paintings of my choice, and come and tell him which one I picked first. I told him I would.

"Billy King-Fraser!" a voice bellowed from outside, snapping Billy and Nana out of the story. It was Rachael, Billy's mom. She was standing in the driveway beside a taxicab, and there were several other people with her. They were reporters and photographers who had been following Rachael around all day. She decided to get it over with, and let them talk to Billy.

"Billy, we have to talk. Come outside," Rachael demanded in a tone that only she could project.

Billy just shrugged, looked at his grandmother, and walked out to meet his mother and the reporters. When he got close enough, he saw the painful look in his mother's eyes.

Sunrise At Two Lions

Chapter Five – Billy's Silence

"I don't remember. I just remember falling though the ice and being really cold," Billy said to the reporters and photographers. "I broke through the ice and crawled back up on the pine needles. I was really cold. That's all I remember until Mrs. Littlefield picked me up and took me back to Nana's."

The reporters from the newspapers and radio and TV stations pressed and pressed Billy for more information, but he had decided to do what his mother wanted and not say anything to anyone outside of the family. She was really relieved.

With that, Rachael took her bags out of the taxi and followed Billy back into the house. She gave her mother a look that her mother knew well. It was yet another victory for Rachael. She got her way, once again. But then, something different happened. Rachael stopped and gave her mother a tight squeeze.

Nana started to back away. She couldn't remember the last time that Rachael gave her a hug, not since Rachael was a girl, not since her grandmother's funeral. Nana felt a tear from Rachael, wet against cheek, but she didn't say anything. Neither did Rachael. She zipped into her room and didn't come out for an hour or so.

When she did come out, she kind of floated. She brushed by Billy, giving him a wink and a rub across his back as she walked by him. Billy smiled at her, and he could feel something very different.

His mother looked softer and more relaxed than he had ever seen her.

"Thank you, Billy," was all she said.

That afternoon Billy came down with the flu. He started getting chills and Nana wrapped him up in a couple of blankets on the couch. But he just couldn't get warm. Then he'd get really hot and sweaty, and throw the blankets on the floor.

Rachael came into the living where Billy was on the couch during one of his hot and sweaty spells. She put her hand on his forehead and hollered to Nana that Billy was, "burning up." Nana resisted, of course, but Rachael insisted that they call Dr. Matthews.

When Dr. Matthews came over, he asked Billy if he had remembered any more of what happened to him during the winter. Rachael and Nana were in the room when Dr. Matthews once again asked Billy this question. He looked at his mother and then at his grandmother. Billy didn't say anything. He just looked down a little and shook his head from side to side a little.

Dr. Matthews told Rachael and Nana not to worry, it was just a flu bug. As for Billy's memory of what happened, Dr. Matthews told them they may never know. He thought Billy might have wandered into the woods and found a cabin with enough food to get him through the winter. The good doctor offered that Billy was probably so frightened that he had put the whole thing out of his mind, maybe even permanently.

Calls and letters and notes came in from all over for a few weeks, but Billy stuck with his story. He just didn't remember anything. He asked Nana not to ask him about what happened for a while, and she reluctantly kept quiet about it. Pretty soon the whole thing just kind of died down. And Billy went back to school.

Now Billy had been a "C" student through most of school, with a rare "A" if he really liked a subject. He was kind of lazy about school, like his father. But when he came back to school after being out for so long, it was like he came back with a new brain.

He got caught up on all of subjects in about two weeks. He got a hundred on his first math test, and when he turned in his first book report, his English teacher accused him of having his mother or grandmother write his report. But they didn't. And Billy took home straight A's the rest of the year.

When baseball season came around, Billy tried out for Little League. He had played for a couple of years, but he was mostly put into right field for the last couple of innings, if his team was way ahead. And if he ever got up to bat, the coaches would invariably tell him not to swing the bat, just wait for a walk.

This year, however, everything changed. Billy could throw almost twice as far as the year before, and the first time he came up to bat in practice, he hit a ball so hard, it almost cleared the center field fence. The center fielder had come way in with Billy up to bat, and couldn't do anything but watch the ball fly 20 feet or so over his head.

And the funniest thing of all was that somehow Billy could really dance. Up until now, he went to school dances, but didn't do much of anything but hang around the soda machine, talk to the other guys who didn't dance, and nurse a couple of Pepsi's until the dance was over. The few times he went out on the dance floor before, were when one of the teachers would push for ladies' choice and Billy had to go dance. But back then he would just kind of shuffle his feet and look down, self-consciously.

The first time he went to a dance, after coming back from his mysterious disappearance, he started to dance by himself almost as soon as the first record started playing. And he was really good. It didn't take long for one of the girls to notice, and he got pulled out on the dance floor in a flash.

So, not only was Billy somehow smarter, he was a better athlete and dancer. He was more coordinated and graceful. Everyone was amazed, especially Billy.

"What the heck had happened to Billy King-Fraser?" Everyone wondered. "He's changed so much, and he seems to always have this little smile," they said. But Billy just said he couldn't remember.

The stories that went around town, Lord in heaven, like you wouldn't believe. Everything from Billy was found and nurtured by wolves or bears, some old hermit in the woods must have found him, he was abducted by aliens, and who knows what else.

People did talk about a glow that you could see around Billy, if you looked just right, around sunset. It was kind of a golden, peach-colored light. That kind of kept the alien abduction story going for a while. But that died down, too.

Rachael was vigilant to keep the tabloids away. She and Billy had a pact, and they both kept it. The only person he told even a part of the story to, for months, was his grandmother. Rachael was beginning to pick up on some the things she heard Billy say, and she certainly noticed the changes in him. And once in a while she would ask him a little bit about what happened, but she always approached the subject pretty cautiously.

Grampa and Ron heard bits and pieces, but it made them both really uneasy, so Billy was careful to only talk to Nana, most of the time.

Rachael felt the need to stick around and stay with Billy after his episode, and she stopped travelling around the world altogether. She and Billy finally got to know each other. He was more like the parent, and she was more like the child. You could see that. But it worked for them, and they got closer and closer the more time they spent together.

Not only that. Rachael and Ron got back together. And this will floor you; Grampa and Billy began to spend a lot of time together. Don't get up off the floor yet, because, Grampa also started bringing flowers home for Nana, every Friday. Really, he did, every Friday he'd show up with this schoolboy grin, flowers in hand. Well, Nana just made the biggest deal of it. She was flabbergasted, and delighted.

The grouch was beginning to become a softy. Probably always had been. A lot of grouches are like that. They don't dare let you see their soft side, because they are afraid that they will be seen as weak, or not taken seriously and seen as an intelligent person. Maybe Billy somehow brought this side out in Grampa.

Ron came over more often than he used to before Rachael came home to stay. And, of course, after Billy's adventure, Grampa never questioned Ron's coming in the house. It was like he just forgot about the past, and Ron and Rachael eloping and all.

At first, Ron would spend all his time with Billy. They'd go into Billy's room or in the living room, if no one else was around. But after a few weeks, Ron would spend a little time with Billy, and then Ron and Rachael would talk. A few minutes here and there, and then an hour, and eventually they'd talk way into the night.

It wasn't long before they were "dating" again. Billy and Nana would cross their fingers and look at each other, each knowing what the other was thinking, every time they saw Ron and Rachael go out together.

Grampa would scowl, then burst our laughing. Nana's eyes would tear up, hearing Grampa laugh again. He had been such a tyrant for so long. Nana knew something had changed in him, too. Maybe Billy's glow was affecting everyone.

And so, early one morning, before Grampa headed off to

work, Ron showed up. Rachael got up, too, which was very strange for this sleepyhead who could sack in until noon. Grampa and Nana knew something was up.

"Can I go wake Billy up?" Ron asked. He was up the stairs before anyone could respond. He came back down carrying Billy, who was rubbing his eyes and blinking. But Nana saw his repressed smile. Billy knew something was up, too. And he was pretty sure he knew what it was all about.

Ron took a deep breath, looked over at Rachael like a lovesick teenager, and announced to them all that he and Rachael were going to get married, again.

Nana let out a whoop. Grampa frowned at what he thought was her unladylike behavior for a split second, then caught himself. He began to nod his headed affirmatively, stood up and literally lifted Ron up out of his chair. Everything stopped. No one was even breathing. Then Grampa actually gave Ron a big bear hug.

"I was thinking that it might be time to winterize the camp," Grampa said, after he let go of Ron. "Rachael, you and Ron have any interest in having the camp, if we make it year-round? It would make an awfully nice home for you kids. And I know Billy loves it out there."

Rachael and Ron just looked at him with their mouths wide opened. Then they looked at each other and started laughing and crying at the same time. Billy joined them in a three-way hug.

"Oh, my God, Daddy," Rachael cried. Now she hadn't called her father Daddy since she was five years old. "We used to talk about that we would live there some day, back when we were in high school together."

Now it was Nana's turn to sit with her mouth opened. She mumbled something about knowing they would live at the camp someday, as she got up to put on some tea. She was back to, to everyone, and you could hear her begin to giggle. It got louder. Then she broke out in funny laugh. And that just ignited everyone, especially Billy.

Can you imagine the joy that must have rung through that house? They laughed until the tea kettle whistle grew loud enough to get everyone's attention. It was like a referee's whistle, and they all stopped laughing, finally.

And you can guess that Nana was about to do a tealeave reading, right? Yup, there it was, plain as the nose on your face, the camp on the lake, and a perfect dollar sign on the side of the cup.

"See. Can you see it? Right there, that's prosperity and a peaceful, loving home," Nana squealed, in that high-pitch voice that went up when she was excited.

Grampa went off to work, and Ron and Rachael went right to work on plans for their new home. Nana, Rachael and Ron took turns saying, "Can you believe it?" to each other. Billy went back up to bed. But he couldn't sleep. His family was back together.

The next thing he heard was a scream. It came from Ron's mother. Nana told her what was going on, and it was Grammie's turn to go hysterical with the good news after good news. Billy got up and came downstairs.

"Did you hear, Billy?" his grandmother asked as she snatched him up in her arms and swung him around.

"Yeah, Grammie, of course. How could I not hear?" was Billy's reply.

"Aren't you happy? Aren't you happy? Aren't you happy?" she kept saying. She wasn't looking for an answer. She knew the answer.

And, as she did almost every time she came across the street, Grammie suddenly remembered that she left something on the stove, and went running back. You could see her waving her arms and kind of dancing all the way across the street and up the front stairs into her house.

Billy asked his Nana if he could stay home from school that day. He was still tired from getting up too early. Now Nana knew that Ron and Rachael were going out to the lake to work on plans for their dream house, and she and Billy would have time to talk.

Nana was pretty sure that this new turn of events would open the way for Billy to tell her more of what happened to him. You know, with Rachael and Ron being busy with their new plans and all. So Nana happily agreed that Billy must be really tired, and should stay home. There were only a few days of school left, anyway.

When Ron and Rachael turned into the gravel road leading down to the camp, all sorts of memories came flooding back. This had been their hideout. And if the truth were known, it had always been their secret love nest.

They parked the Jeep at the bottom of the hill and got out to stroll along the lake, stopping to hug each other tightly, without saying a word, every so often. They didn't need to say anything. They could feel each other's heart pounding.

It was early June by now, and the days were pretty warm. The water in the lake was still pretty cool, though. Even the warm spot in the clearing hadn't reached anywhere near swimming temperature.

"Wow, can you believe it?" Ron said yet again. "We're going to live out here on the lake." Rachael heard him, but her mind had taken a turn as she stopped to look out over the lake. A sudden warm feeling came over her, and her mind was definitely somewhere else.

"What do think really happened to Billy?" she asked quietly, as she looked out on the very spot where Billy fell through the ice. "He couldn't have lived out here for three months. I really want to know, but it just scares me so much when he starts talking about being with God and everything. It just makes me crazy."

Ron just shook his head, as if to say he didn't know. Rachael continued to look out over the water for another minute or so, then snapped out of it. She grabbed Ron's hand and pulled him toward the camp.

They walked a couple of steps, then she let go of his hand and broke into a run. The race was on. She beat Ron by 2 steps, as they hit the porch steps, but he caught her by the waist, and bolted past her up to the door, claiming he had won. It was like they were in high school, again.

When they opened the door, Ron saw all the blankets rumpled up near the fireplace and the cereal box and cans and cups lying on the floor. He looked in the kitchen and saw the oven door open. He wondered for a second who had been there, but then drew a quick breath as he recalled Billy's story about coming back to the camp before Mrs. Littlefield spotted him walking along the road.

Ron tried to think how Billy could have survived at the camp with so little food for so long. There just wasn't enough for him to eat from January to April. Maybe he had found some more food. But where was he all the times Ron came out to look for him? Ron shuddered and shook it off. He figured he'd never know what really happened.

"Billy, your breakfast is getting cold?" Once again, Nana's voice came rounding up the stairs. Billy popped up, thinking he was late for school, and then remembered that he had been given the day to skip. He smiled to himself, and plopped back down.

"Come on, Billy. Don't let it get cold."

"OK, I'm coming."

Nana was waiting. She had just finished watering and spraying her plants. When Billy opened the door at the bottom of the stairs, she hit him with a cool spray.

"Hey, I'm not a flower." Billy laughed. He always woke up in a good mood.

"You're my little sweet petunia." Nana cooed.

Billy just shook his head and smiled, and went over to his bacon and eggs and, yes, the cereal and all. They chatted for a while about his Mom and Dad, and Grampa's surprise, but they both knew what today was going to be all about.

Transformation

We're not caterpillars
Some species
Of butterfly communities
To be released
For sudden flight
As winged beauties
Overnight
Or are we
No photosynthesis
Permeates our beings
Until we've had our fill
Unearths us green
With leafy frills abounding
To burst into bright colors
Until we spill upon the ground
Then come around next spring
Red and gold and everything
No such thing
No pink and peach
Horizon within our reach
We are worker bees
Long live the queen
Or so it seems
But still we dream of
Transformation

t r a n s f o r m a t i o n

Chapter Six – Transformation

"So, you were headed back to the castle, I mean, the house. William had told you about the lions. And you were going to choose a painting to bring to William," Nana began, almost before Billy had finished his last slurp of sweet milk at the bottom of his cereal bowl. Billy grinned a big grin, and even though they hadn't really talked in some time about his story, he picked up on it like it was yesterday:

Well, when we got back to the house and we were about to go past the two lions, I tripped on a rock. Then I heard a deep voice. It was one of the lions, of course.

"You're always so clumsy. Pick up your feet. You're really awkward. All you left-handers are."

William had already gone up the stairs and was about to open the door. But he spun around real fast when he heard what the lion said. He told me not to pay any attention to what the lion said. That's what William said all the time, not to pay any attention to the lions.

I ran up the stairs and into the house. I thought I heard a little roar like a laugh, but I didn't look back. I just ran up to my room and started looking at the twelve paintings. I didn't know which one to pick for a long time. I just kept looking at them and looking at them. Finally, I picked one. And I went downstairs to find William and tell him that I had made a choice.

Like I told you, this was a really big house. I couldn't find him and I didn't see him anywhere. I looked in the library and the den and the kitchen. Then I went out to the big porch. William wasn't there, but Aaron was there. He was one of the people I met when I first came there.

He was sitting in a big overstuffed chair, looking out over the water, listening to some music that was playing from somewhere, and I didn't think he heard me come out onto the porch. I walked up behind him, and was going to tap him on the shoulder and ask if he knew where William had gone, but before I could say anything, he said something.

"Did you pick out a painting that you like?"

I told him that I liked them all, but I had picked one out because William asked me to choose one, first. I started to tell Aaron what the one I picked out looked like, but before I could say more than a few words, he got ahead of me.

"I guess you want to know about the painting called, "Transformation", right Billy?"

That was really weird, because that was the name on the very painting I had picked first. I wondered how he knew which one I picked so fast.

Anyway, Aaron just stood up and started walking out of room. He stopped, smiled, and motioned for me to follow him, and I did. We walked up the stairs to my room and he went right over and took the painting off the wall. He turned it over, and on the back was a little piece of paper with some words written on it. It was a poem, and Aaron read the words to me. They said:

Transformation

We're not caterpillars
Some species
Of butterfly communities
To be released
For sudden flight
As winged beauties
Overnight
Or are we
No photosynthesis
Permeates our beings
Until we've had our fill
Unearths us green
With leafy frills abounding
To burst into bright colors
Until we spill upon the ground
Then come around next spring
Red and gold and everything
No such thing
No pink and peach
Horizon within our reach
We are worker bees
Long live the queen
Or so it seems
But still we dream of
Transformation

After he read the words, Aaron turned the painting back over and handed it to me. Then he asked me what I saw. Before I could answer anything at all, he asked me to look at the painting for five minutes before saying anything.

Aaron was the youngest person there, next to Anna. He was really friendly with everybody and he laughed a lot. I thought he was probably twenty-something. He had blonde hair and was pretty thin. He always seemed to be happy. Sometimes I would see him dancing all by himself, even if there weren't any music playing. And when he was just walking around in the house, or while he was helping set the table or something, he would sing out loud a lot. He couldn't sing very well, but that didn't seem to bother him or anyone else in the house at all. He'd just sing along and make everybody smile a lot.

Oh yeah, and he liked to wrestle. You'd start to walk by him and the next thing you knew he'd have you on the floor or bounce you on the couch. And he always thought that was hilarious.

And he didn't do it just to me. He did this to about everybody, even the old guys. Of course, he was really gentle with them. And you could tell it was a way for him to let people know he liked them a lot.

"It looks like a volcano, or Mars, or something," I finally said. "And there's this new plant just starting to grow back,"

"What else do you see?" Aaron asked.

When he asked me that, I looked back at the painting. And right before my eyes, the colors in the painting slowly turned into this beautiful garden with all kinds of flowers and plants. This happened right while I was looking at the painting. It was like it was alive or a movie or something.

I could see the flowers growing up out of the ground and blooming, and bees flying from flower to flower. I could see this incredible sunrise all pink and gold. There were colors like the colors of a peach, too. It was almost like I could smell the flowers and taste the peach. It was all so sweet and delicious. The whole thing made me feel so happy inside.

As I watched all the colors move and the flowers grow, and watched the bees that kept flying around from flower to flower, I saw the leaves on the trees starting to change color, and then this beautiful ray of golden light came through the branches.

When I saw this happen in the painting, I felt just like I felt when I was in that big light, after I fell through the ice. It was the same feeling I had then, when that happened, with all the wonderful peacefulness inside, knowing that God knows me and loves me. Then I blinked and the painting went back to what I first saw.

Aaron must have seen the look on my face, because he just laughed and laughed and grabbed me, and wrestled me to the floor. I tickled him to try to break free. When he let me go, he just rolled over and over across the floor, like a little kid.

"How did you do that?" I asked him.

He just kind of looked at me funny and asked me what I was talking about. I knew that he knew what I was talking about. I told him what happened in the painting when he asked me to look at it again. Then he plopped down on the bed and just looked at me for the longest time.

"So, you really saw it, huh?" Aaron finally said.

I just shook my head, yes. After that, Aaron asked me to take a walk along the beach with him. As we walked he started telling me about the transformation painting. I asked him if he was the one who painted this painting. He said he didn't paint it, but he knew the artist who did paint it.

He told me that the artist used to walk the same beach we were walking on and, looking out to sea, he would ask God, day after day, why he was driven to paint paintings that he, himself, didn't understand, let alone anyone else.

Aaron told me that the artist told him that, one day, while he was going through his usual ranting and raving about his compulsion to paint, that he finally heard the answer inside. He said it was as if something told the painter that God would make his presence felt to some people who saw the artist's paintings. He said that, one day, some people would feel the presence of God by just looking at this painting.

When Aaron said that, I felt like I knew what God meant when he let the painter know the reason for his compulsion to paint his paintings, because that was what had just happened to me. That's exactly what had just happened to me when I looked at this painting. I felt God's presence, from just looking at the painting. I didn't know a painting could do that, but now I do. I was also pretty sure that Aaron was the one who painted this painting. But he told me that he didn't.

He told me that artists create their art to remind us, just from looking at their work, without words, that deep inside of all of us, even when we are really young, there is a sense that there is something very special about us.

We know it in a way, from when we're really young. We feel it. Sometimes we feel it very strongly, other times it's just a vague feeling. But most of the time, as we begin to grow up, we forget. And some people bury these feelings of being special for the rest of their lives.

It begins to happen when we are told to stop daydreaming, and to pay attention to what we are being told, and stuff like that. When we are taught that we need to be realistic and thoughtful about life, and that's the most important thing about life, we begin to lose touch with this feeling of being special.

It's not that being realistic and thoughtful isn't good. It's just that when we give up our hopes and dreams, and feelings of being special, so we will be thought of as realistic and thoughtful, we risk losing touch with who we really are meant to be.

When we are taught that the most important thing is to be like everyone else, and think like everyone else, and follow the rules like everyone else, we lose something of our special feeling.

When we listen to people who gave up on their thoughts of being special a long time ago, and believe that they know better than we do, we are in danger of settling for a life that has lost it's real meaning.

We can give up on our potential for really enjoying life and lose our gratitude for the beautiful gift of life. Then a time can come when we no longer believe in any new possibilities that life holds in store for us. When this happens, we don't believe in, or hope for, transformation any more.

So we go to school, and then to jobs, and we try to find that missing piece in relationships, and new homes and cars and toys, but still we have this empty feeling. We become like worker bees, going to work, coming home, waiting to die. And we fill in the spaces with meaningless junk. And we know it. But no matter what happens in life, we never completely give up. Our dreams may be buried inside, but they are not gone entirely. The spark remains. It just goes deep inside.

Growing up, when we start hearing that we are a "bad boy" or a "bad girl" over and over, and we are told "no" over and over, we decide that we are not special at all. Instead, we begin to feel that we are not good and special. And something inside of us dies, or at least goes to sleep.

By the time we are just a few years old, we have been convinced that the world we first saw as awesome and beautiful and special and loving, is really not the perfect and loving, benevolent place we thought.

We are taught that it is full of danger, and we have to watch out and be careful all the time. We're told that we have to watch out for so much that can hurt us, and we have to pay attention, and think carefully about what we're doing all the time. And so, after a while we forget how to just be, and just play and enjoy life.

We are convinced that we have to be serious and hard-working to get ahead in this life. We forget that the real source of the incredible energy we knew as children came from our joy at just being alive and part of this wonderful loving place. The real productive energy comes from joy, not grim determination. We were born to enjoy life. We know when we're little. But most people forget.

When we are newborn babies and little kids, we get lots of hugs and we hear grown-ups say how cute and adorable we are. Then when we grow up a little bit, we begin to hear the negative stuff, like how bad we've been for not picking up our toys or silly stuff like that. And it feels like love is going away. It feels like we have lost the love that we saw in everyone's face for so long.

It's not long after that we give up on being special. And we give up hope of ever being special again. But we don't entirely give it up. Something inside continues to knock gently and say, "Yes, you are special. You can transform your life and recapture that wonderful reality of joy and delight."

Some people learn to ignore that little voice almost all of their life. Some others are so beaten down and frightened that they never listen again. And it seems like some people never give up on their dreams. They're the really strong and independent ones. And they go for it, no matter what anybody says or thinks.

Then there are those people who ignore that inner voice for a time. Then at some point in their life, they are drawn somehow to search for meaning, to dream once again, to search for something more, that something they feel is missing in their lives. And they start to long for transformation.

Some people start this search when they are very young. Some people start when they are very old, or even dying. Some search very quietly, and some search passionately. It's different for different people. Some never search again.

Something as simple as watching a butterfly go by can start someone on their search and lead them to their eventual transformation. The sweet smell of a rose, or a Sunday drive, taking in the breathtaking colors of autumn leaves, enjoying a beautiful sunrise or sunset, or looking out over the ocean can speak to someone's heart.

Watching children play, listening to music, feeling a tender touch on the shoulder, or hearing loving words can do it. And even just looking at a painting, can do it.

That is really why painter's paint, Aaron said, even if they aren't conscious of why they paint. They create their art to touch people's heart through what their eyes see and their mind knows intuitively. Their paintings are intended to point the way home to that special place once again.

Artists are guides to bring the viewers beyond just the nice, warm feelings and sensations of the colors of the painting, and into the transformation of their hearts. Like Aaron said, and Picasso said also, by the way, the true artist is one who creates art to express the presence of God in the living world, and invites us to see for ourselves.

Aaron told me that maybe not many artists do this consciously. A lot of them are just making pretty pictures. But some artists know this part about God speaking to people and changing their heart through the art they create. These are the gifted artists. They have received a gift from God, and they know they must share it. They may describe what they do differently, but it's the same thing, in the final form.

Very often, this search for transformation and renewed hope for something more in life, or a chance to recapture their joy in living, comes to people after a big mistake or a very painful experience in their life. A powerful event, even if it creates despair, opens them up to hope, once more. Something insides says that there must be more to life than they've decided to believe. And so they long for transformation of some sort.

Someone who feels lost and hopeless, or has a broken heart, or feels really guilty about something they have done, will sometimes suddenly be released to search for this transformation. It's like they've finally given up and then, when they do, their heart opens up.

When life gets really rough, or some event like an accident or an illness happens, some people decide that they have to change their lives by changing everything around them. They want their life to be different. They want desperately to experience a dramatic change.

It's like a bell goes off inside of them, but then sometimes they don't really look inside to make the change. Instead, they look at the things around them. It's like they don't really understand what is going on, but they know that things in their life are not right, and they want them to be different.

But when they are really desperate, and nothing else has worked, they will go deep inside and open up to a new possibility. Then it is possible for a new reality to emerge, for their perspective to change and for a transformation in their life to happen.

Aaron said that, "Out of the ashes of a volcano, in the middle of rough, harsh, black and gray lava, can spring new life. A tender green plant will pop up overnight. And the garden will come back to life. And then new growth and new beauty will change the entire landscape."

He was talking about something that happens inside of us. Then he told me that all the other paintings and all the other stories of the paintings I would hear would be about this transformation in one way or another.

He told me that some of the people who would talk about the paintings would say some really scary and harsh things, but in the end they would come to talk about the beautiful experience that is part of the human experience, transformation, available for everyone who seeks it.

He told me about how much we change when this transformation happens to us. He said, it's like we become a whole new person. People who need forgiveness, feel absolutely forgiven for everything. People who had all these questions about their life, and about dying, and their relationships with other people, suddenly feel as though all of their questions have either been answered or they have just gone away. What were big important and serious questions become unimportant. They don't matter anymore, or they just entirely disappear.

We look at other people very differently. People who used to upset us, with some mannerism or personality that we didn't like, are now just loved for who they are, and whatever they do. Tolerance, Aaron called it. He said we could even "melt' people. My eyes must have gone pretty wide when he said that, because he burst out laughing when he looked at me. He explained that he meant we could soften people's attitude; like a surly waiter, or rude taxi cab driver, with just the glow that comes from us, and all the unconditional love we feel from this transformation.

He even said that the transformation we can experience makes us better dancers and singers. I wondered about this, because Aaron wasn't really a good singer. Well, I guess he was OK. He was really nice, and funny. I guess he thought he was a good singer, anyway.

He said that young people, still in school, would find their schoolwork much easier and a lot more fun. And then he told me that transformed people are more graceful in the way they move, and are even better at sports.

He explained to me that when we have peace of mind, and we aren't worried about how things are going in our life, or how things are going to work out, that we are more physically relaxed as well, and that lets us move more gracefully.

When we are not concerned with what other people think, we don't walk or move stiffly, we move naturally and gracefully. And that's part of what makes us better dancers and athletes.

Finally, he said that life would take on an easy and effortless flow, because we would have a child-like energy. There would be this sense that everything would always work out for the best. Even mechanical things, like cars and things that needed to be put together would run better, work smoothly, and not break down as much. I don't know how a change of mind and heart can really change how a car runs, but that's what Aaron said.

He told me that William would tell me more about the lions of fear and doubt, but he did say that once we had seen the transformation, we would have no fear and doubt. Our mind would just be peaceful, almost all the time. We wouldn't worry about what we should do, and whether or not we should do something, and how we would feel if we did it or how we would feel if we didn't do something. We would just know and trust ourselves, he said. And we would trust in a kindness in life, in nature, and what he called a "kind creator".

Aaron also told me that time would slow down. He said that we would be able to accomplish lots more in a day, because our energy would be so smooth and consistent. Because we wouldn't spend time worrying and concerned with every little thing, we would be very productive without feeling that we were working as much as we were playing with life. Joy produces productive energy, he said.

It sounded like he was saying that just looking at the painting we were talking about could do this, and then at other times it seemed like he was talking about what had happened to me when I fell through the ice. Either way, it all just seemed natural and true to me. I didn't know why, but I felt like I knew exactly what he was talking about.

Then he told me that the reason for all the different paintings and all the different stories is because different people respond to different images and life lessons. He said he hoped that I would remember the stories well, because there are so many people waiting to hear the stories and see the paintings.

Aaron looked at the painting one last time and put it back up on the wall. As he walked by me, on his way out of my room, he picked me up and tossed me on the bed. Then he ran down the stairs, laughing his head off. So that was Aaron's story about the first painting I picked out. It was really fun.

"Just show them the paintings," he shouted back to me from the bottom of the stairs.

"But how can you show anyone the paintings, Billy, when you don't have the paintings?" Nana asked, finally breaking the captivating spell she had been under listening to Billy.

"Oh, I'm supposed to paint them," Billy said nonchalantly.

"From memory?" Nana said, like she couldn't believe what she heard.

"From God," Billy simply replied.

Well, believe it or not, and not many people would not, but at this point Nana was speechless. Billy then told her that he had a lot more of these stories. He said he had listened to stories from the other people at the castle, one for each painting in his room. Then he asked Nana if she didn't want to hear just one story about one painting in one day. She agreed that this was a good idea. That would give her time to really think about each story.

Billy told Nana that the other eleven people at the castle all talked like Aaron did, about art and music, and God and religion and spiritual things. And he told her that they talked about philosophy and relationships and morals and ethics and about all the choices we make in life.

Well, as you can imagine, Nana couldn't believe her ears. Here was an innocent ten-year-old boy, her grandson, who, only a few months ago thought mostly about fishing and climbing trees and reading comic books. Now, here he was talking to her about the true meaning of art, and about life-changing transformation, and philosophy. She was stunned, as you can imagine.

"Nana, can I go now? I think I'm just going to take a walk out to Panther Rock," Billy asked as he touched Nana's shoulder gently. Nana just nodded acknowledgment. She was already in deep thought about what Billy had told her this morning. So Billy headed out for Panther Rock.

Panther Rock was one of Billy's quiet places, just a couple hundred yards or so away from the house, tucked away on the edge of the woods. It was a rock formation, about ten feet high, that had been discovered by Billy a few years earlier.

He would sit in a little nook and watch as the animals in the woods, including panthers, very stealthily strolled by his hiding place. Of course, there aren't really any panthers in Maine. Billy had a great imagination, as you probably know by now.

He loved the movies, and he often came out of the theater totally into the role of one of the characters in the movie he had just seen. Billy had always admired quiet strength and courage. So if one of the hero characters caught his fancy, he was off and running.

There was something about assuming a role and becoming detached from reality that he liked. He also liked being hidden from sight, watching other people interact. That was another thing that he found very appealing. He thought that being invisible would be a most wonderful advantage, and the thought often crossed his mind.

As he climbed up on Panther Rock he slipped into that quiet place; that silent state of mind he had come to know so well. He had become familiar with it as a little kid, playing alone out in the woods and fields.

He would let his imagination take over, and he would transform into a bold hunter of cougars, wolves and wild boar, and other thoroughly dangerous animals. Sometimes he would become an Indian Scout, moving unheard and unseen as he closed in on a campfire blazing in the night, in the old west.

From his unseen and unknown hiding place, he could listen to plans and learn secrets not meant for his eyes and ears. He became very good at these silent games.

At other times he would become an animal himself, with awesome strength. He would become that panther who would stalk its prey so patiently and silently before making a cat-quick pounce from the darkness.

And many times he would be the pursued. He was an escapee

from prison who had devised some incredibly clever way to spring himself free, and the hounds were on his trail. He would criss-cross the brook a dozen times, leap from rock to rock, and even crush berries in his footprints and on rocks to throw the hounds off his scent.

One of his favorite roles was the role of Robin Hood. Billy loved the stories of Robin Hood. The Sheriff of Nottingham and his men were often after him. When they were, he would hide under the leaves or fallen tree branches, or else climb high up into a huge maple tree and watch the men and their horses ride by him underneath.

But there was one thing that bothered Billy in these games. Whenever he found a hiding place, in the deep quiet of the woods, he could hear the sounds of his excited, short quick breaths. And he knew this would give him away if anyone came close enough to hear him – even if he made himself invisible. How could be become absolutely silent? That was a question he hadn't been able to answer.

So, once settled into that perfectly smooth hollowed out place in Panther Rock, Billy focused on staying absolutely still. Only his eyes moved as he scanned the nearby woods. His hearing was fine-tuned to pick up any sound of movement. But there was not a sound to be heard. No panthers around today, it seemed.

As Billy sat quietly and listened more and more carefully, trying to pick up on the slightest sound, it suddenly occurred to him that even his breathing was absolutely silent.

Before his winter experience, he had always breathed in short quick breathes that he could hear on both the inhale and the exhale. Now he was breathing much more gently and deeply, and his breathing made absolutely no sound whatsoever.

He took a quick look at his hands to make sure that he hadn't become invisible. When he saw his hands, he was both relieved and a little disappointed.

In the next instant something new slipped into his mind. It felt very, very close to the sensation he had when he first entered the light after falling through the ice. He had the most vivid sense that he ever had of really being invisible.

He suddenly remembered, as he knew back then, that who he really was; the Billy deep inside, the Billy he had discovered in the light, was indeed invisible.

He felt more alive, in a sense, than he ever had in his life. In his own way, he knew that there was more to him that his thoughts and senses. He knew that there was also more to him than his physical body. In this moment of becoming aware that his breathing was now absolutely silent, he realized that he somehow went on forever.

It was a fleeting feeling and it passed quickly. But it left a definite glow.

As he sat for several minutes enjoying this incredible sense of freedom and joy, he flashed back to his time with William. William talked to Billy a lot about silence. So did someone else.

Sunrise At Two Lions

Silence

Words can't fly like this
Words grant scant relief
From gut-wrenchings
Words frame and box and shove
Screaming yesterday's torment
Pretending to know tomorrow's
No give me dead silence
Sensuous vision
Attune me with billowy blue's
Impregnating power
Teach me to swim wide-eyed
Into the viridescent
Until I disappear into
Sunsets and dreams
Let me abide in magenta robes
Bleeding sweating weeping
Until mystic labors once more
Give birth to unspeakable joy
Beyond thoughts and words
Leave me speechless
Leave me alone
I don't want your solace
I just want to paint
Paintings from the soul

s i l e n c e

Chapter Seven – Silence

" So you ready for some breakfast?" William asked as he gently nudged Billy's shoulder. Billy heard the question through a sleepy haze and just smiled his usual good-natured waking-up smile. He rolled over, rubbed his eyes and then ran his hands through his hair, giving his head a quick series of rubs. Then a big yawn and he was ready to talk.

"Yeah, I'm starved," he said.

William told Billy that he wouldn't be starved for long. They went downstairs for the usual breakfast banquet, with all of its usual gorgeous color and sweet smells.

Aaron was at the breakfast table and so were a few other people. They all smiled and said their morning greetings. And Billy noticed a particularly warm and friendly smile from Aaron. At that precise moment Billy felt like he had known Aaron for a very long time. Before he sat down, Billy went over and gave Aaron a tight hug around the neck. Everyone looking on just beamed.

Right after breakfast, Billy and William headed out for their customary morning walk. And, as was also customary, one of the lion sculptures had something to say as Billy walked by him.

"Don't let Aaron fill your head with all kinds of foolishness and flowery thoughts. He thinks life is just one big joke."

As soon as the lion spoke to Billy, and Billy turned to look at him, he saw Aaron tying a big towel around the lion's ears and mane. Aaron had the biggest grin Billy had ever seen and Aaron told Billy not to pay any attention to lions. Of course, that was the same thing that William always told Billy. The lion with the towel tied around its head looked really silly, and it made Billy giggle.

Then Aaron whipped the towel off the lion and zipped back into the house with a, "See you later, Billy." It was hard for Billy to take the lions too seriously for that moment. He thought he heard a low roar, more like a grumble.

William had walked on ahead a few steps and Billy ran to catch up. As soon as he caught up, William asked Billy what painting he had picked the night before. When Billy told him that he had picked the one called Transformation, William said that he thought so. When Billy asked him why he thought so, William told him that he had seen the new connection between him and Aaron.

"He's really nice," Billy bubbled.

"And what did you think of his story about the painting?"

Billy told William what had happened as he looked at the painting and then he told William what Aaron had said about the artist who painted it. Billy went on to tell William what Aaron had said about the story of the painting, while William listened patiently to the whole story.

By the time Billy had finished, they had come to the patch of light green moss and Queen Anne's lace. As they sat down, William went back to his tale about the lions.

He told Billy that the lions will say that they don't believe in the possibility of transformation, or more accurately, they doubt that there is any such thing. The truth is, William said, they know people can go through transformation. They just don't want anyone else to know about it, because transformation means the end of their control of anyone who experiences it.

"No more Dunbar and Furman, no more fear and doubt, that's what transformation is all about," Billy said in a singsong rhythm. Then he burst out laughing. William did, too.

"Well, another poet among us," William acknowledged, as he rubbed Billy's head again. "Exactly right."

Billy was in a really silly mood and the thought flashed through his mind that he would be bald by the time he left this place, because William was always rubbing the top of his head.

William went on to remind Billy once more that transformation is real and that fear and doubt are only stone lions that can't do anything to us except talk. And they can only talk if we stop to listen to them.

"Just tell them to hush if they try to bother you, Billy. But, believe me, they never give up entirely. They'll creep up on you sometime and before you know it you'll be listening to them. But as soon as you realize it, remember what that lion looked like with the towel wrapped around its head. Just laugh at them and tell them to be quiet. Walk away. Remember who you really are. Do you remember?" William asked very softly.

"Of course I do, William. I fell through the ice and came here. Don't you remember?"

Well, that little wiseacre remark cost Billy another brisk rub on the head. And he and William laughed and laughed, and then they each put their arms around the back of their heads and lay back on the moss. They were silent for the longest time. They lay there just peaceful and silent, enjoying the sounds of birds and little chipmunks and squirrels scurrying around near them. William spoke first.

"Billy, you have received a very beautiful gift. Only a very few people on the earth really know just what you were given. Only those who have experienced what you have experienced can understand what happened to you. But a lot of people love to hear about it, so make sure that you share whenever you can, however you can.

"It's not only the lions, old Furman and Dunbar, who will try to convince you that it wasn't real, or didn't really happen. But some other people you meet and talk to about this will have no way to understand.

They'll be frightened of what you say. They will think you are making it up and they'll make fun of you, and criticize you, and even threaten you for speaking about it. Just remember the experience. No one can take it away. No one can argue it out of you. You know that. As long as you remember that, fear and doubt have no control over you or your life.

"What can happen, though, is that you can make the mistake of thinking that God will take the gift back because of something you have done or will do that you know is wrong.

That's just old religious myth that is simply not true. God is a God of love, the God you met when you fell through the ice. God will never take the gift back, Billy. It was given to you to share.

If you ever let other people or fear and doubt, or even your own thoughts, begin to chip away at the reality of your experience, it can happen that you begin to believe that you have lost the gift, or that God took it back. Just remember how you came to know that God knows you and loves you. It was your own experience, not some-one else's.

"And just so you don't misunderstand, I'm not saying that it is alright to do something that you know is wrong to do. But we all make mistakes and do things that we come to regret. Sometimes we even do things that we know in our hearts are wrong to do. But as soon as we have a quiet moment to reflect, we are reminded of the good person who lives in us and inside of everyone, we change our minds. And just as soon as that happens, we are forgiven by this God of love, no matter what we have done.

The problem is not what we have done. The problem is listening to the lions and forgetting to tune into our hearts and what we really know deep inside. And what do you now know deep inside, Billy?" William asked.

"That God loves everyone just the way they are, no matter what, and he's given them a special gift," Billy told him. William just smiled at him and kept on talking.

"This is why you are here, Billy, to solidly seal the gift in your heart. This is why you will stay here for a while and listen to the twelve stories and see what's in the twelve paintings.

"You are meant to share this gift with anyone who asks you about it, or anyone who comes to listen to you talk about it. If someday someone tells the story of what is happening to you, people will come to know about this gift from hearing about it. And that may start them on their search for their own transformation.

"They may come to wonder about that empty feeling inside and begin to believe they have forgotten something very special about their life. And they may begin to believe that they really can overcome the fear and doubt, and even go beyond that to the transformation that you know about.

"They might begin to believe that they, too, can experience that light, that sunrise in the heart that you've experienced.

"Everyone who comes to this experience of transformation, comes to it in their own way. And they may think that their experience is uniquely theirs. But the experience is the same for everyone, maybe in different degrees, but it's the same.

"They may describe it differently, because, as you know, you can't really put it in words. You can talk about it, but it must be experienced to be understood. And everyone who experiences transformation speaks of it in very similar ways.

"Some really fortunate people, people like you, who have received the gift and who are able to share it, are still in danger of being snared by fear and doubt at some time in their lives, even after receiving the gift, even though they know it their hearts that they carry the gift.

"They let fear and doubt in again and then, for a time, they keep the gift locked away. They're changed forever, but in a way they are back to being controlled by fear and doubt and what other people think. They haven't lost the gift. They just have stopped opening it. You can help them re-open it.

"How this could happen to someone, even though they have received this gift, will be explained to you by some of the others here at the house. And maybe by some life experiences that you are yet to encounter. So if you don't quite understand yet, just be patient and listen and learn."

When he finished that, he asked Billy if he was ready to go back to the house and pick another painting. Billy jumped up and ran as fast as he could.

As he ran up the stairs and past the lions, he pointed at the one who had the towel wrapped around its head before. Billy grinned a great big grin. This time the lions didn't say a word.

As Billy burst into the house, he was stopped abruptly by the delicious smell of apple pie. He turned and he saw the young girl he had met when he first came to house. She was putting a pie on the kitchen counter. Billy walked over and leaned his nose close to one of the slits in the pie crust.

"Don't get so close that you burn your nose," Anna said with a giggle.

Billy looked up and giggled, too. Then Anna easily read his mind and told him that he could have a piece of pie as soon as it cooled.

Billy had not really spent any time with Anna since he came to the house. She was about his age, maybe a little older, and he was kind of surprised to find someone close to his age at the house.

He started to ask her if she knew about the transformation and the stories of the other paintings, but she just smiled. She told him that he would find out when he picked "her" painting. That bit of news really excited him.

So, he spun around and headed for his room to pick another painting. He realized, as he bounded up the stairs to his room, that he was singing out loud just like Aaron did around the house. He hoped he was a better singer than Aaron, but he didn't really care.

When Billy went into his room, he thought it would be a difficult choice to pick a second painting, but it wasn't. He walked right over to the one with the title, "Silence". This time he took it off the wall and read the poem on the back. It read:

Silence

Words can't fly like this
Words grant scant relief
From gut-wrenchings
Words frame and box and shove
Screaming yesterday's torment
Pretending to know tomorrow's
No give me dead silence
Sensuous vision

Attune me with billowy blue's
Impregnating power
Teach me to swim wide-eyed
Into the viridescent
Until I disappear into
Sunsets and dreams
Let me abide in magenta robes
Bleeding sweating weeping
Until mystic labors once more
Give birth to unspeakable joy
Beyond thoughts and words
Leave me speechless
Leave me alone
I don't want your solace
I just want to paint
Paintings from the soul

Billy put the painting back in its place and went, once more, to find out who would tell him the story of "Silence". He was hoping that maybe this one was Anna's, but as he was coming down the stairs, Vincent was coming up the stairs.

He didn't say a word. He just pointed Billy back toward his room. They walked in and Vincent went right over to Billy's most recent choice and took it off the wall.

Billy expected Vincent to hand him the painting like Aaron had done. But instead, Vincent walked over to the window and looked out over the ocean. He looked at the painting and back out at the ocean a few times. He stood there for what seemed a long, long time to Billy.

Vincent had thick and curly red hair and a ruddy completion.

His clothes were rumpled like he had slept in them, and he tugged at his shirt as talked sometimes. His voice was raspy and he looked kind of fierce and angry most of the time. Billy had seen him pacing back and forth on the porch, almost like he was giving some passionate speech or something. But today Vincent had a real peaceful and quiet way about him.

He finally turned to Billy and came over and sat down beside him on the bed. He handed Billy the painting without saying a word. And Billy looked at this painting called, "Silence", without saying anything himself.

He remembered how Aaron had asked him to look at the painting for five minutes, and he remembered what had happened after the five minutes were up. He kind of expected this painting to go through the same sort of change that he had seen the other painting go through. So he just sat quietly staring at the painting. Neither he nor Vincent said a word for the longest time.

"I see the ocean and I see," Billy finally started to say. But as soon as he started, Vincent stopped him.

"Don't tell me what you see. Tell me what you feel, Billy." Vincent gently interrupted.

"I feel like I'm flying and looking down at this beautiful water." Billy went on.

Once again, Vincent gently reminded Billy to talk about what he was feeling, not just what he was seeing.

"It feels like what I felt when I fell through the ice, when the beautiful blue colors flashed and flashed. They were just the most pretty blue colors I had ever seen. They made me feel peaceful and at the same time they made me feel like there was something more to see in them.

Part of it also feels like I felt when I was banging on the ice and struggling to break through. And it makes me feel like I'm drowning and I'm going to die. But I know I'm not.

"It makes me want to swim hard, to feel the energy and power of the water, to ride the waves and laugh and sing and swim to safety. Then it feels like something or someone is coming to help me, and make sure I make it back to shore. At the same time it feels like something is holding me back. And now it feels all peaceful again.

"It feels like I'm back on shore and laying in the sun and it's drying me off with its warmth. There's something warm and golden that's part of this painting. It's beautiful. It makes me feel like everything in the world is beautiful. There are no words to describe exactly what I feel.

"Now someone comes and wraps me up in this heavy soft robe. It's a deep red color, almost purple. And it's really heavy and warm. It makes me feel sleepy. I feel like I'm ready to fall asleep, but then I remember that feeling of floating in the light. My whole insides are so bubbly and happy. The floating feels like I'm on an air mattress in my grandparent's swimming pool."

Vincent listened and looked directly at Billy without saying a word. When Billy looked up at Vincent, he was kind of startled to see Vincent looking at him so intently.

Then Vincent told Billy about a time in his life when he tried to use words, for years and years, to try to tell people that they could feel in life what Billy had felt in the painting, by just looking at it for a few minutes.

He told Billy about a time when he went to live with people who worked in coal mines deep into the earth and how he tried to tell them about the strange beauty of hard, hard work and coarse clothing and lined faces.

But most of them wouldn't listen. They insisted that the grim circumstances of their lives were anything but beautiful. Vincent said that he tried to tell them of a love of life that knows no circumstance. They didn't know how that could be. They wouldn't listen. They still don't, he said.

So then, he told Billy that he decided to try painting and putting into pictures, the strange beauty he spoke of to these people. To him, it was no different than the real beauty that can be seen in nature, in the sky and in the fields and in peoples' faces. To him this beauty was a beauty that is beyond physical and visual beauty, a beauty that clenches life in tight fists.

Vincent called it the beauty that can be seen and felt in the gut, in sweat and tears, in grizzled faces, in a life of struggling and pained expressions. The beauty of real life, with no perfume, Vincent called it.

Vincent told Billy that he grew up in home where they read the bible. His father was a preacher and he used to tell Vincent that if he would look closely enough, he would find God in nature, and in other people.

Vincent told Billy that he believed that was true and that he tried to find a way to put the truth of it into everything he painted. He painted with this in mind as much to convince himself as to communicate it to others. But he always knew that he painted to express the presence of God in the world.

And he felt that people who knew the experience of God, or were searching for their connection to God in their hearts, would feel this in his paintings, by just looking at them.

Vincent would look out the window most of the time he was talking to Billy and it made Billy feel that Vincent was always looking for something to maybe put in another painting, or find another way to communicate what was in his heart.

"Did you paint all of these paintings in my room?" Billy asked him.

"No, I just try to do my part, Billy. I just try to do my part."

Billy saw a real sadness come over Vincent and he wasn't sure why. He found out when he asked the next question.

"Why did you call this one 'Silence'?"

Vincent was quiet for the longest time. When he finally spoke, he went on to tell Billy how he painted for ten years, trying to capture the essence of life, real life in his paintings.

He talked about being with people in the dark mines and in their homes, and painting pictures of them. He painted in the fields and in the woods, both day and night. He felt driven to paint and to try to communicate what he could not put into words.

One day, he told Billy, while he was painting, and in complete silence, his whole consciousness changed. He wasn't expecting anything to happen, but in the silence, the message he was trying to put into his paintings came through to him in a way he hadn't expected.

It was the same message, in a way, but it was beyond what even Vincent thought it was supposed to be. He described to Billy something very similar to what Billy had experienced. Vincent even used similar words that Billy used to describe his experience. He said he saw these incredible colors, and saw a huge light, and felt God's love and God's presence

Billy remembered thinking, at the time, that what William had said about the experience was right. It's the same for everyone.

Vincent said that he felt an incredible surge of energy and joy from his experience. He called it an experience of deep intuition. He was sure that his paintings would reflect his new insights and, to him, they did.

But years and years went by and he never sold any paintings

or received any recognition as an artist. That wasn't his real goal, but it had an effect on him. Fear and doubt began to creep in; not so much about his ability as an artist, but about his insights and reason for painting. So, he told Billy, he went silent and focused his attention more intensely on his paintings.

Vincent told Billy that he had found something beautiful and wonderful in silence. He found a harmony and a peacefulness in the silence that he couldn't find anywhere else in the world. And he would spend hours sometimes just sitting silently. He would do things like focus on the horizon, or on one of his paintings, or just on his breathing. He said he that sometimes he would put his attention on his breathing rhythm. He would be aware of when he was inhaling and when he was exhaling. He would do it very gently and silently. This would quiet his mind, and in this quiet he would feel God's presence and a peace of mind that was impossible to explain.

He told Billy that he had always had a hard time around people, and often felt awkward and uncomfortable, especially around women.

He started to tell Billy about his troubles with women, but then told him that he was too young to hear about it, let alone understand. So he didn't go into any detail that Billy could remember.

But in the silence, Vincent said, he could feel a sense of balance and comfort. And the more time he spent in quiet time and solitary time, the more he became convinced that his paintings could say more than he ever could with words.

Billy recognized much of what Aaron had told him about artists and why they paint, in what Vincent was saying to him. And he remembered how William had told him that people who had received the gift of knowledge about their connection to God could still be caught by fear and doubt for a while.

This is what Vincent had said to him a few minutes earlier. He was about to share this thought with Vincent, when he heard Vincent say something that was very familiar to him.

"Sometimes I think I would just like to be invisible."

As Billy heard those words, the exact words that he had said to himself, word for word, he blinked and suddenly realized that he was still on Panther Rock. He had been remembering the times with William and Vincent so vividly that he forgot where he was.

He was back home and had come to spend some quiet time on Panther Rock. And he, too, was feeling invisible. He quickly checked to make sure he was back and visible. He was, and so he breathed deeply and stood up.

He didn't know how long he had spent in his reverie about being back at the castle, but he thought it must have been a really long time, so he quickly climbed down and headed back to the house.

When he walked into his house, he saw Nana putting an apple pie slice right beside a tall glass of cold milk on the kitchen table.

"I thought you'd be back about now," Nana smiled.

"Well, you were right, as always, Nana," Billy chirped. He pulled up his chair and started in on his pie. As he took the first bite, the words he had remembered hearing from Anna came to mind.

She had said that she would have a piece of pie for him as soon as it cooled. It seemed like that all had happened an awfully long time ago to him now. Yet, in a way, it was like it had just happened. And here was his pie.

As he was finishing his pie, Nana reminded him about the paintings, and how he said that he was going to paint them. Billy liked to draw and he was always copying cartoons from the paper and his collection of comic books, but he had never done any painting. Billy just nodded affirmatively. He had a mouth full of pie.

"How about if I pick up a paint set for you?" Nana offered. "I'm going downtown this afternoon. Do you want watercolor or acrylics, or oils, or what?"

Nana was really creative and she liked to get involved in creative projects. She even tried her hand at painting a few times. So she was pretty excited at the prospect of seeing what Billy would do. He told her to get whatever she wanted and he would do the paintings with whatever she brought home.

Well, later that afternoon Nana came home with acrylics, brushes and some thick practice paper for Billy. Acrylics are water-based and clean up really easily, so Nana thought those would be best for Billy. He was only ten years old, after all.

Billy was eager to try the new paints and he liked them right away. He liked the way they smelled, and he liked that the paint washed right off his hands with water.

He had watched Nana try some painting with oils, and he didn't like the smell of the oil and turpentine, or the fact that it was really hard to wash off the paint. So he was really happy that Nana came home with these nice smelling paints.

But there was a problem. Billy thought that he would be able to paint the paintings he remembered easily. He was sure that he was supposed to paint them, and he was sure that God would give him the ability to paint them just as he saw them.

It didn't happen that way. It didn't even come close to happening that way. The colors and shapes that Billy created were dark and dense. He had no idea how to put the mix of colors, and the shine and glow in the paintings that he so vividly remembered seeing.

And that was just enough to cause Billy to forget an important lesson he had been taught. When Billy saw that he wasn't able to produce the paintings the way he remembered them, he let just a shadow of doubt in.

Pretty soon he started questioning whether or not he would ever be able to do the paintings he saw so clearly in his mind. Sadly, he even began to let a shadow of doubt creep in about the reality of what had happened to him.

It was just a little doubt. He really knew that he had been given a gift to share. Nothing was going to rob him of his experience. But Billy's glow dimmed ever so slightly over the next few days. And he became more silent.

Devotion

I must leave
I cannot subscribe
To your blind creed
Your blue green feathers
And golden tongue
Will not tether me
I will not become
A parrot in your pulpit
I will not die
Choked by a white collar
Save your wretched lies
You barren robber
Who cannot bear
The mournful sighs
Who gorges on
The blood of Christ
Blind and deaf pharisee
On your knees
Pretense that neither
Knows nor sees
Blasphemy
Cannot lead me home
I must be shown
The ransom note
Devotion

d e v o t i o n

Chapter Eight – Devotion

Now don't think that Billy lost his glow. He didn't. And he didn't lose the effect he had on people. His grades continued to be excellent, he was still a standout athlete, and he could really, really dance. But he stopped talking about what had happened to him as much as did before his attempt to capture the paintings.

Of course, Rachael was relieved, and Nana was perplexed by his silence. Nana was so intrigued with Billy's story, and she was so eager to hear more that it was really hard for her accept when Billy wouldn't talk about his experience so freely anymore.

Nana jumped to the conclusion that she was losing yet another battle to her daughter. No matter how much Nana prodded and hinted, Billy wouldn't tell her the other stories. When she would ask why, he would just shake his head and tell her it wasn't time yet.

He did, however, continue to paint. Pretty soon he forgot about trying to paint the images he saw at his room in the big house on the ocean, the castle. He just painted pretty pictures. He could draw really well, and it helped him paint pretty well.

He copied other artist's work, and he painted realistic scenes, landscapes and seascapes, and covered bridges and sailboats. He used nice colors, that he would see in nature and through the seasons in Maine. But he never painted from his heart.

He hadn't become an artist, yet. And he knew it. He also knew that he wouldn't give up. He would keep painting until his ability as an artist matched his knowledge of that perfect place within. And when it did, he was sure that he would be able to paint the paintings his mind could see. Well, he was pretty sure. He wasn't about to give up, anyway.

One late afternoon after school, Billy came home, determined to work on his skill as an artist. It was a nice day and Nana was kind of surprised that Billy had come in and gone right to his room. She hadn't heard a word from him in an hour or so, and she hadn't heard any music coming from his room. So she had to check in on him.

"Billy, you OK?" came that shrill voice spiraling up the stairway. "Can I bring you a soda?"

"I'm fine, Nana. I'm just working on some of my paintings," Bill reassured her. Nana wasn't about to pass up the opportunity. She grabbed a soda for Billy from the refrigerator and bounced up the stairs like a schoolgirl.

"Oh that's wonderful, Billy," Nana said as soon as she saw what he was working on. Nana always encouraged Billy, and said something positive every time she saw any of his artwork. She had done that since he was a little kid and would show her cartoon drawings that he had done.

"I'm glad to see you so devoted to painting," Nana said as further encouragement. She hadn't meant anything particularly meaningful when she used the word, "devoted". But the word resonated in Billy's heart. He remembered another painting, and the story that went with it.

Billy thanked Nana for her encouragement. But she knew from the tone in his voice, and the look in his eyes, that something inside of him went off in another direction.

Nana knew that Billy wasn't at all satisfied with the painting he was creating. As soon as that thought entered her mind, Billy said just what she was thinking.

He wasn't satisfied. Something was missing. And he was feeling more and more discouraged with his inability to produce the paintings he felt he was supposed to produce.

Yet, something Nana had just said, something that came fleeting across his mind as she spoke that word, devotion, made him believe that he might find his art one day. He asked Nana if she would like to hear another story.

Of course, Nana was really surprised, and she certainly was eager to hear another story. She sat right down on his bed without another word. Billy didn't need a reply, he could tell by the way she was looking at him that she would absolutely love to hear another story from his experience.

It had been at least several months, a real long time, since he offered to tell her another one. For reasons known only to Billy, this is the one that came to his mind, and the one he wanted to share with his grandmother:

I want to tell you about the third painting I picked. I know I haven't told you about the second one, yet. Anyway, it was called, "Silence". And that probably explains it.

But today, for some reason, I want to talk about devotion. You just used that word, and that's the name of the third painting I chose. I think that I need to remember something I was told about this painting.

I was in my room to choose another painting, and I decided on my third choice. I picked it mostly because I liked the colors. It was foggy and raining and almost dark, and I could still see some of the colors in the water and trees. The painting named "Devotion" reminded me of the way it looked outside right then. Almost as soon as I decided that this would be the next painting, I felt someone come up right behind me.

"So, you picked 'Devotion', huh? Well that one's mine. So I guess you'll hear my story of the miracle of devotion next, young man."

I jumped when he said that, because I didn't hear him come into my room. But most of all, I jumped because he knew that I had just picked another painting, and he knew the name of the painting I had picked. That seemed to be the way it always worked.

His name was Jonathan. He was kind of heavy, and he always stood very straight with his shoulders back like a soldier or something. And his eyes were bright blue. He took my hand and shook it firmly. That made me feel really relaxed and peaceful. He walked over to the painting, lifted it off the wall and turned it over. On the back of the painting was another poem taped to it, just like the others. It said:

Devotion

I must leave
I cannot subscribe
To your blind creed
Your blue green feathers
And golden tongue
Will not tether me
I will not become
A parrot in your pulpit
I will not die

Choked by a white collar
Save your wretched lies
You barren robbers
Who cannot bear
The mournful sighs
Who gorge on
The blood of Christ
Blind and deaf Pharisee
On your knees
Pretense that neither
Knows nor sees
Blasphemy
Cannot lead me home
I must be shown
The ransom note
Devotion

Jonathan quoted the verse, word for word, without looking at the writing. Nana turned pale when she heard Billy quote the verse from memory as well, and she looked at Billy with the strangest look.

"And how do you remember every word of the poems, now?" Nana asked Billy. This was the second time he had recited the verse from memory.

"I don't know, Nana. I can just see them. I can see the painting and the words are right there, in my mind," was all Billy could say.

"What do you think they mean?" Nana asked impatiently.

"I can tell you what Jonathan told me about this one, Nana. Do you want to hear what he said?"

Nana said she was sorry for interrupting, and asked Billy to go on with his story. Billy smiled and took one last sip of the soda Nana had brought up to him, and while looking out the window of his room like he was seeing the images of what he was about to share, he continued with his story:

Jonathan asked me to look at the painting for a while. We sat down on the end of my bed, and Jonathan put the painting in my lap. Then he asked me what I saw.

At first it just looked like a lot of colors, like the ocean. Then I saw more. I said it looked like a house at night, and the wind was blowing really hard. It looked like it was cold and dark.

But the more I looked at the painting, the more I could see what looked like angels flying around, and I saw a man way in the background looking out to sea. It seemed to me like he was trying to call to someone, but they couldn't hear him.

It was like when you read tealeaves. I could see a whole story, and the more I looked at the painting, the more the story went on and on.

I told Jonathan that it felt like there was someone or something like a secret that was being kept in the house. I felt as if there were a parrot in the house that would just repeat what people said to it, without really knowing what it was saying.

Jonathan smiled at me and started telling me about his life. He told me he used to be a minister, a preacher, but he left the church because people just didn't get what he was saying, or he couldn't say what he really wanted to say. He said he wouldn't settle for being what he called, "a parrot in the pulpit." You could tell he liked saying that.

Then he asked me if I minded if he talked about Jesus. I told him it was OK, because my Nana talked about Jesus, and Muhammad, and Buddha, and Krishna, and Moses, and a poet named Rumi, and all sorts of people like that a lot.

Jonathan seemed to really like that. He said that people get all funny and weird sometimes, because so much has been said about Jesus that scares people, and makes them upset.

Jonathan said that Jesus was a real person, and a real nice person, not someone to be afraid of for any reason. He was someone you could talk to.

He talked about Jesus, all right. He talked like he knew him or something, like he had conversations with him. He said that Jesus told him that he didn't want to create some exclusive church club that claims to own some special right to their own interpretation of the truth.

He wants us to love and respect everyone, no matter what they look like, and no matter what church or religion they belong to, or what they believe. Jesus just wants us to love one another, simple as that, he said.

Jesus wanted to be heard for what he was really saying, about our connection to God being just like his, but people just wouldn't listen to what he was really saying, Jonathan told me. Jesus did what he said he would do. He is who he said he was. We are who he said we are.

Jonathan said that Jesus was talking about something inside of us that is the most important thing. A kingdom inside, is what Jonathan kept saying. And he kept saying that this kingdom inside is so beautiful, so beautiful, so beautiful. And when we find it, he said, we are in the garden.

If we just take one look at this kingdom inside, we will know what love really is, and how love is waiting patiently all the time, like a flower waiting to bloom. And it's always there for us.

As soon as we remember it is there, it comes right out in full bloom, every time we look at it. It's a beautiful garden that we water with love, Jonathan said.

He said that Jesus taught about how to reach a new level of awareness and come into a whole new consciousness. In this place, we can have an experience of God's presence. We can know, we can experience and be shown how to really, really know what love is all about, in exactly the same way Jesus did. We can know this God of love the same way Jesus did when he was on the earth.

When Jesus said he was the only way to God, he was talking about his experience of God that we can experience in the same way he did. That is the "only way" he was talking about.

It is the experience of coming into the garden, coming into a conscious awareness of what love really is all about. And this truth is the same for all religions and all ways of really expressing God.

Jesus wasn't saying that we had to believe what he said only. He was talking about our awareness and consciousness of God, this God of love. The only way is the way of experience, not parroting someone else's words or even relying on a book, without experience.

He wasn't talking about himself, Jesus, as the only way. He was talking about, "The Christ", which is a, "knowing", a personal experience of the kingdom inside of us as the only way. And he said we all could have the same experience as he had while he was on the earth.

That experience, that "beautiful" experience, Jonathan called it, is the only way for human beings to come to know God. We can't use our thinking mind only, or just believe what someone told us.

The only way to realize that God is real is to experience that God, that kingdom, inside, in our hearts. Then we know that the kingdom within is real and we know that it's not about religion only. It's about experiencing the core, the essential truth of the religion, not our idea about it, or some concept that we set in concrete. That's not it, Jonathan kept saying. That's not it.

Not our ideas, or somebody else's ideas. It's about knowing for ourselves. It's about experiencing God for ourselves. Nothing short of this is real for us. And this is how we can know God is real.

We can't fill ourselves up if we just talk about food. We have to eat it. We have to eat what the true spiritual masters have for food. Jesus told his disciples that he had this food that they didn't know about, but that he wanted so much to share with them, and with us.

Eating this food that Jesus was talking about is what really nourishes us. And when we are nourished with this food, we realize the kingdom within. We realize that what we really want to do in life is, first of all, be a kind and loving person.

It's about being kind and loving, and being good to people – to everyone. Faith and belief point the way, but the experience of God in your heart is the, "only way", that Jesus was talking about, to really know love.

Jonathan said that a lot of other religions and spiritual paths, and lots of other men and women, know what Jesus was talking about, and know it in the same way that Jesus knew it. That's what Jesus wanted us to know, and still wants us to know.

"Jesus was not originally named Jesus Christ," Jonathan told me. He said that "Christ" is the experience of God in our heart. That's what Jesus knew about and what he wanted to teach others. "Christ is the experience of God", Jonathan said over and over. That's why people called him Jesus, The Christ, and later Jesus Christ.

Jonathan said Jesus is really sad that people use his name and act like Jesus is part of their exclusive club only. Jonathan said that Jesus is bigger than that. He came for the whole world, not just part of it. He told them he had other "sheep", that they didn't know about.

Jesus wants peace on earth, for all men and women, everybody. How could he want an exclusive club that judges and condemns other people? That's not what Jesus did and that's not what he taught, either.

He told us that experiencing The Christ would show us plainly that God loves all people and we would know for ourselves that God doesn't want us to call other people wrong, or not love them, because of what they believe.

Jonathan said that a lot of people who call themselves Christians, are not true Christians at all. They are scared and empty, and they become "parrots in the pews" without even really knowing what it really means to be a Christian. That's because they don't know what else to do, and they have been so manipulated and robbed by "parrots in the pulpit", those who don't really understand what the real teachings of Jesus are all about.

It's like artists who just paint and sculpt, and create their art without any real connection to what art can be. These are not yet artists in the spiritual art sense. They are copiers, more like the parrots who speak beautiful words, but don't realize the meaning, deep in their hearts and souls.

Artists can paint wonderful pictures; just like people can say wonderful words. They can actually touch other people's hearts with their work and their words. But when they become artists in the true sense, the real joy in what they do will come through.

Then the artist who creates the work and the people who see the work will see it in an entirely new light. This is really hard for some people to understand.

People know when they are genuine in their art and their religion, and they know when they are not. People know when they have received a special gift from God. There's no way to mistake it. And they know when they have not yet received it.

Sometimes they fake it. And sometimes they settle for head knowledge, a concept of God, in place of an experience of God.

Some of these people are so scared that other people won't think they are good Christians, that they are the people who start fights and persecute other people, saying they are doing it for God. They are the very sort of people Jesus was so mad at when he lived on earth.

And, just like the people Jesus blasted, they have hard hearts and deaf ears. Not much has changed in two thousand years, Jonathan said. Some people talk the talk, but not all of them walk the walk. Hate still doesn't cure hate. Only love cures hate.

Then Jonathan talked about the painting again, and told me that the man shouting was him and others like him. People who have experienced the pure joy of coming into God's kingdom, while they are alive and here on earth, want very much to share this experience. It becomes the central and over-riding purpose of their lives.

He said that these people are, "forerunners", of a special kind. They are the people who are brave enough to proclaim what they know to be true from experience. And there will be more and more of them to come, until the world changes.

Jonathan said that a day would come when the whole world would know about this beautiful garden and the world would live in peace. It won't be a time of converting everyone to one religion or one world order, or anything like that, he said.

It will be a change of heart that the whole world will feel. It will come in a torrent, like a flood. Suddenly, people all over the world will begin to know the presence of God in their hearts. Everyday more and more will come to know until it spreads over the entire world. Then there will be no more room for hate and violence and terror.

Future generations will wonder when they read of wars and

acts of terrorism. It won't make any sense to them. They will all be loving and kind to one another, all over the earth.

No one will go hungry. No one will be poor and have to go without anything. The world will still offer abundance, and all people will be seen as equal. People will share everything, gladly and joyfully. And they will wonder why it was ever any different. The last thing Jonathan told me was that a lot of people still want desperately to be rescued from their negative thoughts and belief in what other people have told them.

So many people have been kidnapped and robbed of what is their natural birthright; peace of mind and happiness, by people who Jesus called, "False Prophets". Jonathan liked to call them parrots. Parrots in the pulpit, he would say over and over. He'd always have this fierce frown when he said that. And then he would beam with a big smile, like he liked his own joke.

The man in the painting calling out to sea is calling to these people who have been robbed, but who can hear him, even ever so faintly. If they will listen to what he is really saying, he will rescue them from sadness and fear and the feeling of emptiness. This is the meaning of the ransom note in the poem. The whole world will be ransomed from the darkness of fear and doubt. This will come.

When I asked Jonathan what the title of the painting meant, he told me that "Devotion" is a choice that we come to when we really find out for ourselves what our life is truly about.

Devotion comes and gets us, he told me. Devotion gives us incredible energy and joy. It is through people's devotion to always showing the character of God's love that they have been shown.

The wish to be ransomed comes to people at some point in their lives, when they face up to the fact that they are feeling empty or sad or guilty, or all of these things. And they decide to do something about it, even if they don't know yet what it is.

Jonathan talked about how, when we are feeling lost or unfulfilled, we start trying to figure out what these feelings are all about. And we change jobs and change partners and think it's all about money or material things.

But when we finally recognize that our feeling of not being content and happy is really is about not knowing who we are and what we are in this life to do, we will sooner or later start on the path to discovering the miracle of devotion.

Our initial devotion will be to finding out how to fill the emptiness, how to achieve peace of mind and happiness, no matter what. When we come to that point in our life, we will know it. And when we are just stalling and denying that we feel empty and lost, we know that, too. It doesn't matter what we say to others, we can't kid ourselves forever.

One day, deep devotion will find whoever makes the choice to look within, and not give up until they know for themselves that there really is a kingdom within, waiting to be rediscovered.

Then Jonathan asked me to take another look at the painting. When I did, I remembered what had happened to me when I fell through the ice. It was all right there, everything he said. I knew exactly what he was talking about.

I had experienced the kingdom within, in a flash. I couldn't believe it was happening again. It felt so wonderful. It all came back as soon as I looked at the painting. I started smiling, and then I looked up at Jonathan.

He had a great big grin on his face, and he hugged me really, really tight for a long time. Then he put the painting back up on the wall, turned around and looked at me. He asked me if I thought I would ever be able to tell anyone about the story of this painting. I knew I could. But Mom doesn't want me to talk to anyone about what happened to me. She doesn't think people will listen, or they'll think I'm crazy. So I can't tell anyone.

"Well, you're telling someone, Billy. You're telling me." Nana said very softly, almost in a hoarse whisper. "Go on."

Billy went on for just a little bit, because he remembered that Jonathan had told him that he had to leave the church because everyone got so mad at him when he would ask them to tell them about when they came to know God.

He asked people, when they came up for communion, to tell him the date and time and everything. And a lot of people couldn't. So he wouldn't give them communion.

He'd tell them to pray and seek to know God, through what Jesus really taught, and then they would really be Christians, and they would know it for sure. Then he would give them communion.

"That would make a lot of sincere believers really upset today, Billy. There are many, many people who believe in God and believe in Jesus, and who try to live moral and ethical lives. They consider themselves good people and good Christians," Nana said when she heard this.

She had a real concerned look on her face. She was beginning to understand why Rachael didn't want Billy to tell anybody else about what had happened to him.

Billy told her that he knew that, and he knew that they were really good people, but Jonathan had told him that they had settled for a lot less than Jesus had for them. And they knew it.

But if they had this inner happiness and peace of mind that the inner experience of Christ consciousness brings, then they had come to know what Jesus really had for them. And they knew when they did not really have that, too.

Billy told Nana not to worry, that those who knew, knew they knew, and those who didn't know, knew they didn't know. He kind of chuckled when he said that, because of all the "knews" and "knows".

He repeated several times, at this point, that he was just telling her what Jonathan said to him. But Nana had noticed that sometimes it sounded like Billy was talking about what he had been told, and other times he talked as if he were the one doing the talking.

As soon as he finished telling Nana about his third choice of a painting, and the story from Jonathan, he turned around and picked up his paintbrush. He thought that now, after telling Nana the story about the painting named, "Devotion", he would be able to devote himself to his painting, for sure. But before he even dipped the brush into a paint color, he was staring out the window, and drifting back in time.

He heard, "People will laugh at you if you try to tell them what Jonathan told you. They'll think your some kind of Jesus freak or something like that, another self-righteous hypocrite. What do you know, anyway?"

The lions were at it again. Billy and William were just coming down the steps after breakfast, ready for their customary morning walk and talk. William cleared his throat, and the talking stopped abruptly. Billy started to run ahead, but William sat down on the steps between the two lions and called Billy to come back and sit down beside him.

Billy started walking back kind of slowly. He was beginning to really not like those lions at all. He looked at their frozen stone expressions, expecting one or both of them to start their usual put-downs. But they were silent.

"They won't say anything while I'm right here," William told him. So Billy sat down.

William rubbed Billy's hair, like always, and pushed down on one of his shoulders in a playful way. Then William jumped up and started running down toward the beach. Billy knew a race was on and he quickly ran after William, passing him just as they stepped onto the sand.

As they walked, William asked Billy what he thought of Jonathan's story about the painting and poem that he had picked. Billy said he liked it, and it made sense to him, and he was working on the devotion thing.

"Do you know what it means to be devoted to something or someone?' William asked.

"Sure. It means you are really, really serious about something you want to do, and you won't give up on it. And it means you really, really like someone a lot. Like you're devoted to them."

William loved the way Billy responded, and it made it really easy for him to further explain what the word, devotion, meant in Jonathan's story. He told Billy that he was right on the button. People who are really, really serious about finding peace of mind and enjoying life, will become devoted to finding a way to do it.

Just like people who want to learn to do something really well, like play the piano, or learn another language, or become an artist; they must be devoted to practice and learning. But there's more to it in Jonathan's story, he told Billy.

"If people in a Christian culture come to really know what Jesus and other enlightened teachers really taught, and they come to the experience of the kingdom within that he talked about, they will turn their devotion to sharing what they have come to know.

"And in many ways they will become devoted to the teacher who came to them, in gratitude. They will understand that he or she really did ransom them from fear and doubt, and bring them into a kingdom of peace of mind and joy in life.

"If their knowledge and experience came from another religion, or not any particular religion at all, but from an enlightened teacher, then their gratitude would evoke this feeling of devotion to the source of their experience.

"Many enlightened teachers are not really looking for devotees. They are lightbearers who simply wish to pass on the light to others, for them to share. If some people find great comfort as a devotee of an enlightened teacher, the teacher will not usually turn them away. But as Jesus said, 'The student is never greater than the teacher. It is enough that the student becomes as the teacher.'

"The joy that comes from receiving the light creates a heart that wishes to serve and encourage others toward this wonderful realization. The more that we share the light we have been given, the brighter the light will become. Eventually it will be bright enough for the whole world to see. This is what will come from devotion. It is this devotion, this appreciation, and this joy of service, that strengthens us in our walk through life, and encourage others to seek what we have found.

"A commitment to not let anyone take away from us what we have received, and the deep trust that what has happened to us is genuine, will keep us from being completely robbed of our joy ever again.

"So, devotion, in this sense, means just what you said. It means you never give up. You don't let fear and doubt, and what other people think, stop you from being devoted," William said .

Billy's ears perked up at the sound of the words that William used; fear and doubt. And Billy chirped away at another rhyme.

"Never listen to fear and doubt, that's what devotion is all about."

William laughed, and agreed. Then he went on to make another point with Billy. He explained how some people will become passionately devoted to a concept or a cause, and sometimes become so strong in their commitment and cause that they forget to be kind and loving.

This particularly happens to people who do not have the inner knowledge. They just have the book knowledge or belief in what they heard. With the heart knowledge, kindness and love come as part of the package. With the head knowledge comes the ego and pride. It's a delicate balance.

"I know. They become the parrots that Jonathan was talking about," Billy piped up.

"Well, I guess we got that covered," William said.

"Yup," was Billy's reply, simple as that. Billy said that "Yup" out loud as he was thinking back to this time at the castle. That was enough to bring him back to his room and his painting. He still had a paintbrush in his hand, and now he had a new determination to paint.

Elation

As a dark heavy fog
Stalks a clear day
Lays in wait for prey
Diminishes my world to gray
I entertain painterly visions
Ferocious brushes
Thrusting verdant lush fields
Yielding red and gold harvest
Rich passionate exciting
Sensual colors more enticing
Than sienna paps
And burnt umber mounds
Waves of wet paint
Blushing unexpectedly
Creating discreet blends
Making sounds as sweet as
Those of friends in love
But I am not hopelessly lost
Although the cost my sanity
I have a painter's vibrant vanity
Endlessly blissful reverie
Rapturous creation
Of a mountain high
Elation

e l a t i o n

Chapter Nine – Elation

S o Billy was ready to go to back to his painting with a new sense of purpose, determination, and devotion. But it still didn't work out. Even though he worked really hard at it, and thought so carefully before adding a color, he couldn't bring the paintings that were so clear in his mind to life.

By the time summer ended and Billy was getting ready to go back to school, he had put his paints away. And he stopped mentioning anything about his experience or the stories of the other paintings. He didn't know if he ever would.

Of course, a lot of other things were happening in his life. His Mom and Dad had almost finished remodeling the cabin to make it year-round. And Billy and Grampa had helped them a lot. So they had been out at the lake most of the summer.

This gave Billy and Grampa time to fish and just hang out together. Grampa wasn't much of a talker, and Billy liked the quiet, so they were pretty good fishing buddies. They'd row out on the lake and each drop a fishing line in the water, and sometimes just sit there for a couple of hours without saying a word.

Their fishing lines had little red and white plastic balls tied on them about six feet from the end of the line, with the hook and bait on it. The ball, called a "bob" would float on the surface of the water, with the hook hanging down in the water. This way, when a fish nibbled on the bait, the floating ball would bob up and down and they could tell that they had a bite.

If it was a good-sized fish, the bob would go right out of sight under the water and they could feel the tug on the line. When that happened they knew they had a good one; a bass or a pickerel.

So, day after day, Billy and Grampa would sit there, just staring at the bob on their line until they got a bite. Well, one day, while they were out on the lake, Grampa ventured a question. Now this wasn't like Grampa. He didn't ask questions. He liked barking orders. But he couldn't help notice that this summer, Billy didn't chatter constantly like he used to when they would fish.

And even at home, Grampa had noticed that Billy would sit quietly, sometimes staring out the window for the longest time. Grampa used to get after Billy for his fidgeting all the time. He used to yell at Billy to, "Park it," when Billy was too restless. But Billy's new quiet unnerved Grampa almost as much as the fidgeting.

So this one day toward the end of summer, out on the lake, he happen to ask Billy what he was thinking about. As much as it might surprise you to hear that Grampa asked him a question like this, Billy's answer is sure to surprise you even more.

"I was wondering if you knew God, Grampa."

Now this wasn't a subject that Grampa was real comfortable with. He tolerated Nana going to church and thanking Jesus out loud for something once in a while. But this was different.

"I don't trouble myself with that a whole lot, Billy. I'm just a pretty practical and down-to-earth type. So I just take care of what has to be done, and get along as best I can, and I don't really think about it. Doesn't really matter to me one way or the other if there's a God or not. I'm just a simple working man. Never had much to do with religion or any of that stuff," Grampa told him.

"Well, what do you think happens when we die?"

"We just die, Billy. It's like going to sleep, only you don't wake up."

"And that's it?"

"That's it. Now let's get back to fishing, OK?" Grampa finished the conversation with a stern finality in his voice. Or so he thought. But Billy had more to say.

"Is that why you used to be so mean all the time, because you think we just die and that's it?"

Well, that made Grampa just furious. Of course, he had been a terror, for years. But in the last few months he had softened a lot. Billy's prodding brought back the old grouch in a split second. That happens sometimes. He told Billy to get his line in, and while he was doing that, Grampa rowed back to the dock like a madman, without another word.

When they got back up to where Grampa's truck was parked, Grampa threw his fishing gear in the back, got in his truck, and drove off. He didn't wait for Billy, and he didn't say good-bye.

When Billy got back home at his grandparents that evening; Ron dropped him off, his Nana was waiting right at the kitchen door.

"What did you say to Grampa? He's really upset. He said he wants you out of the house. Billy, what did you say to him?" Nana asked him over and over.

Billy didn't answer Nana's question. He just told her to call his father and have him come back and get him. He went on to tell his grandmother that he was ready to move out to lake with his mother and father, anyway. They had talked about it, and Billy was thinking that he wanted to stay with his grandparents for another school year. But this quick turn of events changed his mind.

So Billy went up and packed a few things while he waited for

Ron to come back and get him. He stayed in his room so his grand-father wouldn't see him. When he heard the Jeep pull back into the driveway, he grabbed his bag and came downstairs.

Nana ushered him out the door without a word. Ron was just on his way in, but Nana shook her head and motioned for them to just go. Ron looked a little puzzled, but didn't ask any questions. He took Billy's bag and gave him a quick tug on the shoulder, kind of a hug.

"So, what's up, Rascal?" Ron asked as they got into the Jeep. Billy shrugged his shoulders like he didn't know.

Nana went into the living room to tell Grampa that Ron had come and picked up Billy. Then she said she wanted to know what was going on, but Grampa wouldn't say another word. All he told her was that he wanted Billy out of the house.

He called him a pretty bad name, and Nana did hear him mutter something like, "Calling me mean. That little...Don't I bring you flowers?"

Nana thought to herself that the truth hurts. Of course, she didn't say anything. She had seen these outbursts plenty of times. She knew he'd get over it after a while and everything would be fine again. Ron and Rachael were planning to get re-married in just a few weeks, so she hoped he would be over it by then and not spoil the wedding.

Nana felt really bad to see the old grouch emerge again, after a few months of relative peace in the house, and even a few gestures of genuine caring from Grampa that she hadn't seen in many years.

Grampa even started talking about changing his mind about giving Ron and Rachael the cabin. But Nana told him that the deed was already signed over to them, and he couldn't do that. Grampa said he couldn't remember signing any deed over, but Nana assured him that he had. Actually, he hadn't. Nana took care of that in a few days, and forged his signature, telling the bank that he was too sick to come in.

It took Grampa about a week to calm down. He even skipped his Friday stop at the flower shop that week. He really couldn't understand why Billy's comment had upset him so much. Of course, he thought it was the comment about being mean that upset him. But that wasn't it at all.

It was when Billy asked Grampa about God and about dying, that's what really upset him. Grampa had a real deep down fear about death. He had decided when he was much younger that there's no kind of God. He felt sure in his mind that God was just something people made up to help them with their fear of death.

So this bitterness crept into his life, slowly and surely. He was convinced that life was, for the most part, a struggle that ended with death and darkness, and that's it.

He lived in fear of death. It wasn't a constant dread, but it was there. It is for lots of people at times, but Grampa never seemed to be able to get past it. Maybe something he saw when he young. Anyway, Billy had prodded his grandfather's fear with the questions.

Billy didn't realize it. He was only eleven years old by now and to him there was no question about the reality of God. He had experienced the presence of God. He had absolutely no fear of death. It didn't even occur to him to be concerned about it. He had already been given a glimpse of heaven.

His question to his grandfather came from the early stirrings within him to share this knowledge, even if he wasn't mature enough to recognize the impact these stirrings would have on other people, just yet. Of course, in one way he already had more maturity than many people ever reach in their lives.

So now the King-Fraser family was back together. Billy had

come to live with his mother and father in their home on the lake. Just a little detail of Ron and Rachael getting re-married, and everything would be in place. Only as the days went by, it didn't feel that way to Billy. He was kind of sad. He missed living with Nana, and funny as it may seem, he missed his grandfather.

Nana came out to the lake a few times, and she called Billy every couple of days to make sure that he was doing all right, and to find out if Rachael was feeding him well. Nana would bring a box of goodies with a lot of the things that she knew Billy liked. Nana especially made sure to bring him a good supply of his favorite, apple pie.

Truth was, Rachael hardly cooked at all. Ron did most of the cooking, and he and Billy did the shopping.

Nana told Billy that as soon as the wedding was over, she was sure that Grampa would have forgotten all about being mad, and as a matter of fact, was already saying that he missed Billy bringing him his slippers. Billy laughed when he heard that, and it made him feel a lot better.

Nana and Rachael worked on the wedding plans when Nana came to visit. Nana was hoping that Rachael and Ron would have a nice church wedding this time, because they eloped the first time. But Rachael wanted to have a small outdoor wedding by the lake.

So you know Rachael got her way. Nana was just happy that Rachael agreed to have a caterer and a photographer. Billy heard Rachael say to Nana not to make such a big deal of the wedding. He heard his mother say that a few times, and it surprised him a little, but he didn't think too much of it at the time.

Billy was too young, at the time, to pick up on it. But his mother was having some real second thoughts about re-marrying Ron and settling down. Seems she had met someone in Florida a few months before Billy's disappearance, and hadn't given up contact with him.

Ron was oblivious to Rachael's uneasiness. He was so happy to have his son back after he thought he had lost him for good. And then he was delighted beyond belief that he and Rachael got back together. Now with the home on the lake just about ready for year-round living, life was wonderful as far as he was concerned.

So Ron was shocked with what happened just ten days before the wedding. He came home to find Billy sitting at the table staring at a note that he had in his hands, with this blank look on his face. Ron was used to Billy's quiet times, but this was different, he could tell.

"What's up, Rascal?" Ron asked him.

"I got a note from Mom," Billy answered. His voice was very quiet. He looked up at his father, and Ron could see that there were tears in Billy's eyes. Ron didn't have a clue. He chuckled as he spoke, thinking maybe it was some kind of joke.

"You got a note from Mom?"

"Yeah, you got one, too."

Billy pointed to a small white envelope with "Ron" written on it. As Ron was opening the envelope and wondering what the heck was going on, Billy clued him in.

"She's gone, again."

Rachael's note went on about how sorry she was, but she had made a big mistake thinking that she could settle down in Maine. She knew the timing was terrible and all, but by the time Ron would be reading this note, she would be on a plane back to Florida. She wouldn't be coming back. The marriage was off. It had all been an emotional roller coaster for her, and she had been caught up the emotion. And she said she was sorry.

Ron tried to hide his reaction, for Billy's sake. But he was devastated. The first time he and Rachael had agreed to split, they had spent months talking their way through it and he came to accept it gracefully. Now, all he had was a note in his hand, ten days before he was to re-marry his childhood sweetheart.

To him, this coming event was to be a dream come true, from a more mature and grateful perspective. He had embraced the idea of the family reunion with all of his heart. And this caught him way off guard. He was so sure that Rachael felt the same way as he did.

To say he was stunned would be to put it way too mildly. He was floored. Later his feelings were to turn to red-hot anger. But for the moment he took a deep breath and held it together.

"Well, ain't this a kick in pants, Rascal?" Ron said bravely.

Billy just shrugged his shoulders. He wasn't really sure how to react. He had seen his mother come and go every few months for as long as he could remember. And, of course at his age, he wasn't nearly as emotionally invested as his father. And he had other things on his mind to deal with.

Only a few weeks before, he had been pushed out his home of the last few years and had to come and live with his parents. So, on top of the separation from a very close relationship with his grandmother, he was now separated from the mother he was really just getting to know.

"So am I going back to live with Nana?" Billy asked.

Ron didn't answer. He didn't even hear the question. Old Queenie, the Irish Setter, seemed to pick up on the quiet sadness that had come over the house, the way dogs do sometime, and came over to nudge against Ron. He sat down on the couch, just looked out at the lake and gently stroked Queen's head and back.

Ron wasn't lost in thought. He was more like he was lost in silence. It was like he wasn't thinking at all. He just sat there and stared out over the lake until it got dark.

Billy fixed himself a sandwich, like he was used to doing since coming out to the lake, and went into his room. He started to turn on the small television Ron had hooked up in his room, but decided not to watch television. Instead he reached for his paints. But he didn't paint that evening.

He packed his paints, brushes, and all of the practice paintings he had done in couple of grocery store bags. He also rounded up the few paintings he had done on the small canvas boards Nana had bought for him. And then he took all of it to the tin trash can out back, and dumped it all.

"There, with all the rest of the garbage," he said to himself. What he was thinking, of course, is that he had wasted his time trying to paint, and that he'd never be able to paint the paintings he had seen. He'd even forgotten what most of them looked like. And many of the lessons he had been taught were yet to be learned by experience.

He hadn't talked about his special experience for a while. His mother made sure of that. He really didn't know how to approach anyone but his grandmother about it, anyway. He hadn't been able to paint what he remembered. And now he felt like an orphan. He wasn't with his grandmother, his mother was gone, and he didn't know what would happen to him or his father.

The very worst part of that evening is that Billy felt abandoned by God. His glow dimmed to the point where he didn't recognize it. He wondered what he had done to cause all this pain. He felt like he was being punished. He took the whole thing upon himself, even though he was only eleven years old. Kids do that sometimes. His world had turned to gray.

Billy stayed with Ron. That turned out to be a pretty bad decision. Ron started drinking and smoking pot to ease his pain and forget about Rachael. He brought home friends who talked to Billy while they were stoned, or in a drunken stupor, and filled his head with their foggy views and bitter assumptions about life.

By the time Billy was thirteen he was getting high with Ron and his friends. And before he turned fourteen, one of Ron's girl-friends introduced Billy to the joy of sex. From there, things just got worse. Billy lost interest in school, in sports, and never even considered painting, unless he was high. And then his stoned efforts would quickly create dark and muddy paintings that he would throw out before they were finished.

Nana never suspected what was going on with Billy. To her, he was still the fair-haired young boy who could do no wrong. She did-n't like his long hair and his negative attitude, but she mostly kept that to herself. Billy's grandfather had long ago agreed to reconcile with Billy and allow him in the house. But he hated Billy's long hair and he wasn't quiet about it one bit. Billy pretty much avoided him.

Once in a while Nana would venture over into the time of Billy's disappearance and his story of what happened to him. Billy would just dismiss it and tell her that it was long ago, and just the vivid imagination of a young boy. He had managed to bury the whole episode pretty deeply. Just like he was burying the guilt of what was happening out at the camp.

Every so often, though, Billy would catch a glimpse of light coming through the trees, see the innocent look in a young child's eyes, or hear music that would bring him back ever so close to his time of elation. It would stir some old memories, and sometimes even touch his heart briefly. But his guilt, the old lions of fear and doubt, kept him locked tightly in their grip, at least for now.

Actually, that "now" turned out into years and years. Billy managed to finished high school, and even took some part-time ourses at the University of Maine in Augusta. He worked at a lot of different jobs, waiting on table, selling furniture, driving a cab.

By the time he was in his early twenties, and still living out at the camp with Ron, and he seemed to be pretty settled into a life in Maine. He had no real ambition to travel or do anything special with his life. Day just drifted into day, and he stayed slightly high or drunk much of the time.

One evening, out at the lake, Ron and Billy and a bunch of their friends were partying. It was toward the end of January, and they had built a bonfire on the edge of the lake. Most everyone was skating on a section that they had shoveled off after the last snowstorm.

Billy was off by himself, a little bit to the side and had skated through some of the soft snow. The snow packed up under one of his skates and he came to an abrupt stop. As he fell hard against the ice, he heard it crack. That sound hit him like an electric shock.

He stood up shaking so badly that he could hardly skate to the edge of the lake by the fire. He sat down, took off his skates, put his boots back on, and headed up to the house.

He was still shaking, almost like a cold shiver. And he had this awful feeling of dread. He had a warm drink and sat down on the edge of his bed, but he couldn't stop shaking. And the dark feeling just got worse and worse.

That night Billy dreamt of his time at the castle. This was the first time he had revisited this place, in his mind, for many years. But there was William, and Billy as he was at ten years old.

They walked along the beach for a long time, just strolling along and enjoying the day. William watched Billy run ahead, and stop to throw a rock out into the water. Billy would run and jump, and spin in the air. And William would just smile, and feel those tender feelings of love that he enjoyed so much.

A fog started to roll in and William called to Billy that he wa
heading back to the house. Billy ran to catch up with him as the
headed back.

The next thing Billy saw was the bright fourth painting he ha
picked, way back then. He saw the verse as clearly in his dream as h
had when he first read it.

Elation

As a dark heavy fog
Stalks a clear day
Lays in wait for prey
Diminishes my world to gray
I entertain painterly visions
Ferocious brushes
Thrusting verdant lush fields
Yielding red and gold harvest
Rich passionate exciting
Sensual colors more enticing
Than sienna paps
And burnt umber mounds
Waves of wet paint
Blushing unexpectedly
Creating discreet blends
Making sounds as sweet as
Those of friends in love
But I am not hopelessly lost
Although the cost my sanity
I have a painter's vibrant vanity

Elation

Endlessly blissful reverie
Rapturous creation
Of a mountain high
Elation

"It feels really peaceful, like I'm on a walk out in the field. The grass is really thick and soft under my feet. I almost bounce along as I walk," Billy was saying to himself as Bernie walked into the room.

Billy had taken the painting called, "Elation" down from the wall. He was wondering about who would tell him the story that went with this painting, when Bernie showed up. Billy didn't hear him come in, and when Bernie spoke, Billy thought for a minute that the sound came from the painting. That really startled him. But then he turned around and saw Bernie.

Bernie was a tall, thin man with a smile on his face that just seemed to be his natural expression. He walked slowly and gracefully all the time. Billy used to see him out on the beach, hitting golf balls into a circle of rocks he had made.

Billy would watch Bernie hit a dozen or so balls into or near the circle that was about thirty yards down the beach, and then walk up to pick up the balls he had hit. Then he would start over and do the same thing, over and over and over. Billy thought it sometimes went on for hours, but it was probably on few minutes at a time.

"Can't you just feel the plush grass under your feet?" Bernie had said when he came into Billy's room.

"That's just what I was thinking," Billy said, in an excited voice, like he was surprised that Bernie had said exactly the same thing that he was thinking. Of course, by now, not much surprised Billy about this magical place and the magical people in it.

"That's just what I was thinking," Billy said out loud as he sat up in bed. It took him a few seconds to collect his thoughts and realize that he had been dreaming. As he lay back down on the bed, he could recall the painting he had seem in the dream in explicit detail.

The colors were bright and fresh, and he could envision them in a way he had not been able to do for years. He began to recall the story that Bernie told him, and how he had reacted to the painting.

"So what else?" Bernie asked him, simply as that.

Billy described the feeling he had walking through the field and into the woods at home. He talked about how he loved to lay down in the thick green grass and sink into it, and feel the warm summer sun on his face. It made him feel safe and protected as he lay there looking up at the sky. As he would look up in the sky he would imagine that he could fly.

He told Bernie about how he would tie a big towel around his neck and pretend to be a Superhero who could fly to the rescue of anyone in trouble.

Bernie laughed when he heard the part about pretending to fly. Bernie told Billy that this painting reminded him of flying over a beautiful golf course. And Bernie said that for him, hitting a golf ball high, high in the air and watching it soar gave him the same feeling. Bernie said that he could feel himself flying like the golf ball and it was a wonderful feeling. It was like his spirit soaring, and coming close to God.

That made golf a magic game for Bernie. Every aspect of it reminded him of the wonderful creation that he was part of, as he walked along the fairways. He even loved it on his occasional walks into the woods to find an errant golf ball.

He felt close to God when a shot landed close to the flagstick

And when he successfully putted the ball into the cup, and watched it disappear, he could feel himself go deep inside to a place of tranquility and satisfaction with everything about life.

"You know what that feels like don't you, Billy?" Bernie said as more of a statement than a question.

"Yes, it feels like everything in the world is beautiful, and God's love is so beautiful. It makes you just want to tell everyone about it," was Billy's bubbling reply.

Billy looked back at the painting as he spoke. He saw what he first thought of as a sun shining, but the more he looked at it, he thought he saw a spaceship with lights that were brighter than the sun. It looked like the spaceship was flying across the sky.

Then, right before his eyes, in much the same way the transformation painting began to move as his looked at, this one began to move. Only this one went in an entirely different direction.

When he saw what looked like a spaceship start to move, he thought was just staring at the one spot too long. But then is was as if the lights went out in the spaceship shape, and the whole painting turn gray, like a black and white photograph.

When Bernie saw his expression, he asked him what he was feeling. Billy told him that the painting had turned to gray, and it made him feel really sad. He said it was like he was being left alone and he couldn't feel the love around him anymore.

"You can bring those colors back if you concentrate, Billy. Just look through the eyes of the artist, look with a painterly vision. Imagine the colors as you saw them. Look around the room and out of the window. Pick up the colors and put them back in the painting," Bernie said to Billy in a very soft and soothing voice.

Bernie went on to tell Billy that sometimes in life, even if we're not fully conscious of it, thoughts will come drifting in and try to turn our world to sadness, and fear and doubt.

He asked Billy if something came into his mind as we w:
looking at the painting, before it turned to gray, but Billy said he di
n't remember anything other than thinking the shape that he first sa
as a sun, looked like it might be a spaceship.

"How did you feel when you thought it might be a spac
ship?" Bernie asked.

"It scared me for a second. I've seen movies," Billy started t
say. But Bernie stopped him in mid sentence.

"That's all it takes, Billy. That little sliver of a thought that h
a trace of fear in it. As quick as that, fear can turn your world to gra
And once it catches hold, it will try to tie that scared feeling to anoth
er time you were scared or sad. Once you listen to fear, it can take yo
on a mind game that robs you of your joy for a time."

"The secret is," Bernie said, "to stop listening to the scare
voice, or the sad voice, and stop watching the images that are gray an
colorless. And the way to do that is to focus on what you are seeing
either around you or in your mind's eye. But either way, once yo
begin to tune into the magic of colors, their joy will come to you.

Find something with bright colors to look at, or rememb
something with bright colors and just drink those colors in. Colo
have a natural joy in them. Focus your attention on them, and mak
them brighter and warmer and richer.

Keep doing this until your painterly vision returns. You'
know it has returned when you feel your heart lighten up, and you
spirits brighten."

Billy started looking out at the water, and then he looke
around his room. He looked at the other paintings, and then h
looked at the red sweater that Bernie was wearing. His expressio
began to change and a smile came back.

"Wow. That works!" Billy announced loudly, as if he had just found a new treasure.

"How do you feel right now?" Bernie asked him.

Billy said that the peacefulness and joy and feelings of love that is all around came back to him. And when he looked at the painting that he had chosen, the colors were back. This time when he looked at the bright yellow and gold shape, he said he was sure it was the sun.

"Let that sunrise come right from your heart, Billy. Whenever you feel like your world is turning gray, go inside and begin to bring that sunrise up. Find it outside and find it inside your heart." Bernie told him.

Bernie talked about really bad things happening in life, like people dying, and accidents that hurt people really badly. He told Billy that, of course, these really tragic events can turn your world to gray so much that it feels like the color and the joy will never return. But the joy of living can always return in time.

Some things in this life are just impossible to understand, and some things we just have to let go of and turn over to a power that is greater than we are as individuals. Some things we just have to leave to God, and trust in his divine plan, as hard as that can be sometimes.

Over time, we can look back and see how even something sad and tragic has made us stronger and more aware of the importance of being a kind and loving person. You can see that when something bad happens in a family or a community. People draw closer. There hearts and kindness and compassion come to the forefront. They experience love in ways that can really surprise them.

Another thing that can really take the color out of life, Bernie went on, is guilt. He carefully explained to Billy that even though he didn't understand it right now, he would learn that maintaining good relationships between people, in business and in social life are a very delicate balancing act.

We can hurt people with our tongue, by what we say, and we can hurt people with our own self-concern and our selfishness. We even hurt people we love very much, and it is almost impossible for them, or us, to understand and accept. But we all do it at times. It's part of life.

We can get caught up in emotions and excitement and do things in the passion of the moment, that we never dreamed we would do. And when the guilt catches up to us, it is one of the cruelest robbers of joy of all. When we know we have hurt someone, it can haunt us and hound us mercilessly.

"The lions, again," Billy said out loud, meaning only to think that thought.

"The lions, absolutely right," Bernie replied.

"William told me about the lions," Billy let him know.

"He knows about the lions, that's for sure," Bernie responded. "Don't ever forget about the lions, Billy. They are very sneaky. You can control them. You can overcome them. You can live without fear, and find incredible joy in living. But they are always lurking, and waiting for an opportunity to sneak up on you. So just remember what William is teaching you."

Billy listened and watched as Bernie went back to the painting and picked it up. Bernie began talking about a strange and powerful energy that is both beautiful and dangerous. As he thought back, Billy knew that Bernie had been talking about sexual attraction.

"It's beauty and attraction is that is feels so incredibly pleasing, like nothing else we experience in the physical. It can't be put into words. The soft and tender intimacy, the loving emotions and unique physical sensations feel very close to the spiritual feelings. They are so pleasant and exciting that the urge to enjoy them over and over can entice us away from almost anything.

"And while it is so beautiful and attractive, it is also the source of much of the hurt feelings, and guilt and shame that people feel. It is so complex, that people don't talk about it a whole lot. And a lot of people carry secrets about their feelings and things they've done, and the shame they feel their whole lives.

"The power of sexual attraction, and the way we respond to it, is one of the lions most potent weapons. They offer convincing arguments to bring fear and doubt into people's minds, whenever they feel guilty about their response to this energy. The lions are quick to accuse and tell people that they have done something to make God turn away from them and not love them anymore.

"But you know that God is a God of love and forgiveness. You can beat the lions, even at this game. William will tell you more about this another time.

"And anyway, Billy, you'll understand a lot more about this when you are older. I just want to remind you to focus upon the colors of the painting, the colors of the world, at a time when you feel gray, or tempted to do something you know is against your conscience. Let the colors bring joy.

"As you let your awareness of vision become the focus of your thoughts and senses, you will feel a joy and a gratitude for the gift of vision. The fact that you can see colors will strike you with awe, much like that of a child's delight with something so simple. You will touch those feelings deep within that let you know you are more than just your feelings and senses.

"You will find these feelings powerful enough to bring you back into the awareness of God. And this awareness, this feeling of being in the presence of God's love, once experienced this way, is even more fulfilling than any of the sensual pleasures."

As Billy came out of his daydream and back into his room he brought the memories of Bernie talking to him about physical attraction and this powerful energy that is both beautiful beyond belief and as destructive as dynamite, at the same time.

Billy smiled and winced as the impact of those words caught up to him. At twenty-three, he knew much more of what Bernie had only hinted at then. But there was a lot more to this explosive issue to come into Billy's life. We all deal with this one.

Billy was just getting up to take a shower, dress and go to work, when the phone rang. No one else was up to answer the phone and Billy wasn't sure who was around. So he stumbled out into the kitchen and grabbed the wall phone.

As he reached for the phone, the ice-cold tile of the kitchen floor gave him a bit of a jolt. And before he even heard the hysterical voice on the other end of the phone, that sense of dread he felt when he heard the ice crack the night before hit him like a bad fall. A chill went through him, right to his bones.

"Hello," he said anxiously into the phone.

Ron's mother was on the other end of the phone. She screamed into Billy's ear that he had to get his father and come right down to the hospital. There had been an accident. Nana had been struck by a car, and had been left on the side of the road, outside all night.

It seems Grampa had fallen asleep in his chair in the living room in the early evening, and Nana suddenly remembered that she hadn't checked the mail that day. It was just starting to get dark, and as she ran across the street to the mailbox, the driver of a pickup truck didn't even see her as he came over the rise just before the big hill.

He had been drinking and thought he must have hit a dog or a tree branch or something. Either way, he didn't even stop. Nana was found at about 4 am by another early morning driver who just happened to glance over to the tall grass on the side of the road. He caught just a glimpse of a slipper, but it was enough to make him stop. That's when he found her. He ran into Nana's house and rushed to the phone to call the police and an ambulance.

Grampa heard the racket and woke up in the living room. He was startled by the noise of the man hollering into the phone, and it took him a minute to remember where he was. He looked for Nana, first and then heard the man who had found her talking into the phone. When he heard what was being said about a woman in the road, he ran outside and saw that it was Nana. He started to run toward her, but fell to his knees about ten feet away from her and couldn't bring himself to go any closer.

The sound of a police siren approaching snapped him out of it, and he walked toward Nana as the officer jumped out of his cruiser and knelt down to check Nana's pulse. She wasn't breathing, and there was no pulse. He looked up at Grampa and shook his head just as the ambulance pulled up.

Grampa stood stone still as they gently lifted Nana onto a stretcher and put her in the ambulance. They said he didn't move from that spot until all the people and cars and police had left. Finally, Ron's mother drove him to the hospital.

Now she was normally very cool under pressure and not much of anything upset her that much. But this was too much, even for her. She repeated herself, saying exactly the same thing she had just said, a second time to Billy on the phone.

Billy leaned against the kitchen counter and started to throw up in the kitchen sink. Ron had heard the phone ring and was on his way into the kitchen when he saw Billy leaning into the sink.

"Hey, Rascal, overdid it a bit, huh?"

When Billy turned around to look at his father, his eyes were already red and swollen, and tears were streaming down his face. Ron knew that there was something much more serious going on than just a few too many beers.

"Nana is dead," Billy wailed. The words hit Ron's ears like a sledgehammer blow. "Gram called from the hospital. She wants us to come right away." Those were the only words Billy could manage before a wave of unspeakable sadness came over him.

Ron and Billy dressed in anything they could find and flew out the door. Ron motioned that he would drive, but by now, in just a few minutes, Billy had settled down and had a peacefulness about him. So he asked Ron to let him drive.

The drive to the hospital was silent for a while, then Ron wanted to know if Billy knew any details. Billy told him that Nana had been hit by a car, that was all he knew. Ron shuddered.

When Ron and Billy walked into the hospital emergency room entrance, Billy's grandfather and Ron's mother were right there. She was standing beside him, with her hand on the top of his head. He was slumped in a seat with his face buried in his hands, and you could see his body shaking and tell that he was sobbing heavily.

"She didn't make it," Ron's mother said softly. She told Ron and Billy what the police thought had happened, how it must have been a hit and run. Ron hugged his mother tightly and Billy sat down next to his Grampa and rubbed the back of his shoulders. Then Billy said something that made Grampa let out a wail.

"Nana's in a good place, Grampa. She's with God now. She's in heaven."

No sooner had those words left Billy's lips than he felt a jolt in his gut that he hadn't felt since the time he heard the ice crack, back when he fell in and froze.

In a split second he found himself back in time, back at the entrance to castle. At least he thought it was back in time. He was just reaching for the door when it opened. It was young Anna who opened the door. Only Anna was now a beautiful young woman, about Billy's age.

When Billy saw her, he realized that he had not gone back in time. The time was now. He was twenty-three. Anna smiled sweetly and told Billy exactly what William had told him the first time he showed up at the castle.

"We were expecting you, Billy."

As Billy stepped into the kitchen, he was hit with that same delicious aroma that he knew so well. Then he was hit with something else that took his breath away.

There was his grandmother, Nana, big smile on her face, beaming, holding a piece of apple pie in one hand and cold glass of milk in the other. She didn't see Billy. She was just setting the pie and milk on the table.

As soon as Billy saw her, he blinked and found himself back in the hospital, still rubbing his grandfather's shoulders.

"What do you know about, God? How could your God let this happen? " Grampa cried out. "What do you know?"

Billy knew that he would have plenty of time to answer his grandfather, and he knew that now he would not keep what he knew he knew to himself any longer. He felt a surge of renewed passion.

Billy told his grandfather that he was going to come to live with him, again. His grandfather just nodded his acknowledgement.

He wasn't expecting any answer to his questions. He didn't believe that there were any satisfactory answers. Billy knew that there were.

Passion

Blood red invades
A darkened stage
The rage begins
With a stabbing wound
Shrill screaming silences
A searing breath
As the blood suddenly
Turns to gold
Black violent storms
Return as blue
Blue no longer blue
Attuned with green light
Night after magical night
This transcendent flight
Every night every night
Until at last the mystic
Visionary missionaries
Who obstruct the view
Renew the sacred vow
What have they to do
With me who will die
With me who sees
Who knows who is right
The passion of the maestro
Who creates this opera life

p a s s i o n

Chapter Ten – Passion

If Billy hadn't had that glimpse of Nana at the castle, right after she died, he might have been really guilt-ridden about not sharing more of his castle experience with her while he could. But that brief moment convinced him that not only did Nana know what he had experienced in many ways, she now was part of that experience.

To Billy, there was no question in his mind that Nana was in heaven, anymore than there had been a question in his mind about the reality of God, since his fall through the ice and entrance into the kingdom.

He had let his mother and other adults keep him quiet when he was ten years old. His own doubts began to creep in as he found he wasn't able to reproduce the paintings that he thought he was supposed to do.

Of course, the lions of fear and doubt had fed Billy that concept, and it worked. But now a new passion flowed through Billy and he was not about to apologize for what he knew, anymore.

Billy took all of the responsibility for arranging Nana's funeral. He was even able to track down his mother, even though neither he nor Ron or anyone in the family had heard a word from her in more than ten years.

Seems a friend of his mother, from high school, had received

a reply from one of their classmates when they sent out reunio
inquiries asking if anyone knew the whereabouts of several of the
classmates. When she heard about Nana's accident, she called Billy
grandfather.

It took some convincing on Billy's part to get his grandfathe
to agree to notify her, but he finally relented. Billy called her. Sh
started crying when she heard Billy's voice on the phone, and sh
moaned a prolonged and painful, "no", when Billy told her what ha
happened.

The funeral was attended by several hundred people who ha
known Nana, as family or friends, and as beneficiaries of her kindnes
and charity through the years. Grampa was a total wreck. He coul
hardly speak to people, and when he did manage to speak it only too
seconds before he completely broke down. Billy stayed by his sid
most of the time.

Rachael looked like she was twenty years older, rather than th
ten or so years she had been absent from the scene. Even thougl
Nana's hair had hardly any gray in it, at age sixty-seven, Rachael wa
nearly completely gray in her early forties. She did slightly better tha
Grampa, but she obviously had a very hard time with Nana's death.

Ron and Billy's paternal grandmother, whom he calle
Grammie, were quiet and withdrawn. And they wore extremel
pained expression. Nana had been a big part of their lives as well.

The night before, Billy had picked up Rachael at the airport
She approached very tentatively, but Billy opened his arms to her. Sh
ran into them, held on tight and cried for a full two minutes befor
standing back and looking at her grown son.

"Thank you, Billy," she said softly and meekly. They botl
knew what she meant, and it didn't need any further discussion. The
drove to Grampa's house without saying another word. Their time t

alk would come later.

Rachael and Ron's eyes met as she and Billy came through the door. Ron looked away as Rachael started to walk toward him, and she urned to Ron's mother. She reached out to Rachael and pulled in her or a hug.

Toward the end of the funeral service, Billy stood up and walked to the front of the church. As he turned to speak, he seemed o cast that glow people used to talk abut when he was younger. His voice, usually soft and slow, boomed as he spoke these words:

Nana and I were really close. She protected me, pampered me, and, yes, spoiled me rotten. She also protected you and pampered you, Grampa. And you, Mom. And even, you, Dad. Do you remember how many times she shushed us, so Grampa wouldn't hear us, just to keep us out of trouble? How many times did she sneak you in late, Mom? As many times as she did me, you think?

And I want to see a show of hands. How many people here have tasted a piece of Nana's apple pie, or been given a whole pie? Most of you, I see. I thought so. I bet that there are people here to whom Nana gave a coat, or shirts or shoes, or money for food. Sure, I knew that, too. Nana touched a lot of lives. She sure touched mine.

I don't know how many of you remember, or know, about the time I was lost. I was only ten years old and I went through an extraordinary time. It was more than I could comprehend at the time. But they told me that I had been missing for three months, ninety days, when I just showed up walking along the road. Mrs. Littlefield found me and took me to Nana's. I see a lot of head nodding, so I guess a lot of you remember that time.

Shortly after I came home, I had a rush of memories about what happened to me, that were very unusual, to say the least. I talked to my family about it. And, except for Nana, well, they freaked out. I really didn't understand why it shocked them and upset them so muc back then, but I understand better now.

If you'll bear with me for just a little bit, I'll try to explain t you how this relates to my grandmother. I hope you will see why th is the time and the way in which I choose to pay tribute to her and t honor the memory of this very special woman. She will always be i my heart.

You see, Nana was the only one who had the courage to hea and an enthusiastic interest in hearing what I needed to say. Again, didn't understand why back then, but I do understand much bett today.

My father and my grandfather gave up on a precious part c life a long time ago. I don't know why, and they probably don't eithe I don't think it's necessary or even important to know why.

As for my mother, I'm not sure why she was so adamant abou keeping me quiet. I knew she didn't want to be embarrassed, and knew she thought she was protecting me from criticism and ridicul Now I have a feeling that it runs a lot deeper than that.

But Nana couldn't wait to hear my story. Of course, if yo knew her, you know that she fancied herself something of a mysti and a fortuneteller. Anybody here have their tealeaves read by Nana Just about everybody, I see.

So, let me go back to that time when I was ten. I was out a Tacoma Lake, ice fishing with Dad. I went out to the outhouse late a night, and I got turned around when I came out.

Instead of walking back to the cabin, I walked out on the lake I happened to walk out on the spot where the sun beats down in a lit tle cove during the day. It must have softened the ice, or melted it jus enough, so that when I stepped on it, it gave way, and I fell through

I tried to fight my way back up through the ice, but I couldn't find where I had fallen through, and I blacked out. Now, I'm not going to take this time to tell you all the details, right now. But I can tell you that I will be talking about it in detail, with passion, from now on!

I had what today is called a "Near-Death Experience" by some people. But let me tell you something, right now. It wasn't a near-death experience. It was a life-changing experience.

It was even more than that. It was a life-after-death experience. I learned beyond a doubt that we are created to know a life of peacefulness and joy, and a life filled with love. I was given a look at heaven, as far as I am concerned.

I came into the presence of God. I found out that God lives right in our hearts. God lives in my heart. God lives in your heart. We carry that presence of God with us, every moment. And we are capable of fully realizing that presence, right here, right now, in our lives, today.

God lived in my grandmother's heart. That kindness and compassion you knew from Nana, that was part of God's expression in her life. And there's no doubt in my mind or my heart about the reality of God. No one is going to keep me quiet about it, again, as long as I live. My heart is filled with so much love and gratitude right now.

I know that may be awfully hard for you to understand. I loved my Nana very much. I will miss her terribly. I feel anguish when I think of the way in which she died. And yes I feel some anger toward the man who struck and killed her with his carelessness, and who then drove away.

But I know that even this man did not intend for this to happen. He made a mistake, he used very poor judgment, and he I'm sure he will pay for it with his own self-condemnation. I feel badly for him, for what he is going through in his mind as well.

But I don't mean to say that he should not be held accountable and be brought to justice by our social and legal system. He should be held accountable. I just don't want to carry hatred in my heart toward anyone. I choose forgiveness.

The love and gratitude in my heart is for the time I had with Nana, and for the assurance that I have that Nana is in a beautiful, peaceful place. I'll call it heaven, OK? You can call it whatever you want, but it is a real place.

I can see that some of you are starting to get uneasy now. My family certainly did when I tried to tell them about it. The only exception was Nana. She was so eager to hear about it. She loved to hear the stories about my experience.

She heard stories that none of you have heard. And she loved them. I wish I had told her more of them. But somehow, I know now that she knew them even without hearing about them from me. And I'll tell you how I know that.

You see my grandfather over there? He is so shattered by Nana's death. He will never be the same. He's not listening to a word I am saying right now. He is all torn up inside and he's only listening to voices of fear and doubt, and the guilt and regret that they breed. But he'll listen to me over the next few months and years. I'll see to that.

You see, Grampa doesn't believe in God. He thinks Nana is just gone, and that she is in blackness and unconsciousness, just dead. Just dead. But I know differently. If you don't believe that is possible to know, then you don't. But you're wrong.

When I came to the hospital, right after they found Nana, Grampa and my other grandmother were there. I sat down beside Grampa and put my arm around his shoulders. To try to make him feel better, I told him that Nana was now in a good place, with God, in heaven.

You know what, that made him really mad. He barked at me, like he had so many times before. Only this time he tried to tell me that I didn't know anything about God. Not only that, even though Grampa says he doesn't wrestle with the question of whether or not God exists, he asked me how God could let this happen.

Do you see the incongruity here? On the one hand, he says there is no God. On the other hand, he obviously has a concept of God; otherwise, how could he blame God for letting this happen, if he doesn't believe in God?

I'd like to just take another minute to respond to Grampa's question about how could God let this happen. God didn't do this. A man who had been drinking and driving a truck did this.

Nana was crossing the street. A machine, weighing tons, was in the control of a human being. Human beings let this happen. The trunk is an object in the physical world. This happened in the physical world. Why do we need to blame God?

"Why did this happen?" is a better question. But that one goes beyond the scope of our understanding. We have no choice here. We have no answers here. We must turn this over to God, to an understanding greater than ours. We must.

What we mustn't do is let this tragedy make us bitter and angry at God. If we close our hearts to God, we become much less than we are intended to be. Because if we close off our hearts to God, we close off our hearts to other people, and we seal up our kindness and caring and compassion. We replace it with anger, and pride and selfishness. That helps no one. Do you think Nana would want that?

So, let me finish by telling you how I know that Nana is with God. The moment I spoke those words to Grampa about Nana being

with God, when we were at the hospital, I flashed back to the time
was with God, exactly in the same way I was with God when I was te
years old. I had another glimpse of heaven.

And Nana was there. She had piece of apple pie and a glass
cold milk for me. She was happy and smiling. So keep that image
Nana happy and smiling, the way you saw her so often when she wa
here with us. I know I will. Thank you for listening.

By now the church was absolutely silent. Some people wer
crying, but others were sitting there dumfounded, wide-eyed, wit
this incredulous look on their face.

People began to file out, and you could hear the whispers ou
side. Billy watched them go. A few people glanced back at him an
turned away. Quite a few smiled at him. And a few others came u
and hugged him or shook his hand and told him that what he had sai
was beautiful.

Grampa didn't leave his chair. He just sat there staring out th
window one minute, dropping his head into his hands the next. As h
tried to make his way to his grandfather, Billy's mother grabbed hi
sleeve.

"I know that was for me, Billy, " she cried. "I have so much t
be grateful for in my life."

"It's all right, Mom," Billy said as he touched the top of he
head.

Billy took his grandfather by the arm and helped him outsid
and into the car. The funeral possession made it's way to the cemetery
Billy wasn't finished. At the gravesite he recited a poem from memo
ry:

Passion

Blood red invades
A darkened stage
The rage begins
With a stabbing wound
Shrill screaming silences
A searing breath
As the blood suddenly
Turns to gold
Black violent storms
Return as blue
Blue no longer blue
Attuned with green light
Night after magical night
This transcendent flight
Beyond mere mortal sight
Until at last the mystic
Visionary missionaries
Who obstruct the view
Renew the sacred vow
What have they to do
With me who will die
With me who sees
Who knows who is right
The passion of the maestro
Who creates this opera life

Billy vowed at that moment to be true to his vision and to never let his view or his passion ever again be obstructed. He had something to say and he was going to say it, and say it, and say it — with passion. As he went silent, the words he had spoken resonated in the air, and in more than a few hearts that were present. For some, they opened a door. For others, the words were meaningless and even confusing.

On the way back to Grampa's house, Billy and Grampa drove along in silence. Billy was behind the wheel. As he reflected on the passion of his eulogy, and the poem that came to mind at the cemetery, he heard a voice speak. He didn't hear it audibly. He heard it within. And he knew he was at the castle once more. It was a very different visit this time:

The voice belonged to Wolfgang, and Billy was suddenly back at the house on the ocean, the big house that he often referred to as a castle. Only there was something very different this time.

Billy was "watching" Wolfgang talk to Billy when he was ten years old. And Billy was listening as a young adult, now twenty-three years old. This time it wasn't like the dream he had, that morning of the chilling phone call about Nana's accident.

This time he felt like he was really there, not just dreaming. It was as vivid as it had been on his earlier visit, back when he was ten. But this time, it was like he was a third person in the room.

It's hard to explain, but Billy at twenty-three could feel what he remembered Billy feeling and understanding as a ten year old, and at the same time he could feel and understand as a young adult, in the present moment.

"So you've decided to live with passion, Billy. That's an excellent choice. Passion is what brings color and music to life. As you grow older you will understand more and more of what this painting and poem are all about. And you'll certainly grow to understand much more fully what passion is all about.

"Passion can be incredibly powerful and rich, bringing an enjoyment to the life experience that is unknown to those who are afraid or unable to feel passion. Those people settle for a gray life.

"If the lions have successfully convinced someone to shield themselves from passion, by being reasonable and rational at all cost, the costs are great. The costs are much greater than they will ever realize, and their life will be dull and stressful in great part.

"Unless they are rescued by someone with the power and passion that only an experience of the presence of God can give, they will settle for much less than their life is meant to be.

"Of course, there are passions, so called, that are violent and ugly. These are passions of the ego and intellect, not passions of a loving, kind and compassionate heart. These are not the passions of which music speaks. The sound of music is a joy to the heart.

"Even popular music, of all sorts, has this beautiful message. When your heart is open and you are in that magic place, every song is about God's love for us and our reciprocal love for God that comes from the times that our hearts are touched by God's presence.

"There are times that our love for everyone and everything in life is right there in the lyrics so clearly that we wonder why we didn't hear it before. But our heart and mind have to be in that place of harmony that produces music. Our heart and mind can resonate to the sound of the music and the message of the lyrics so powerfully that we can be lifted up into a place of indescribable joy and peace of mind.

"You will experience times, Billy, when every song you hear will have the same message. And there will come a time in your life when you will know that you are on earth to share the message of the indescribable joy that you have known. How you will do that, in art in music, in whatever you do in life will become clear as you mature.

It seemed to Billy that he was being brought back to the castle, not only to remember what he had been told before, but to re-live the experience through the eyes of the young adult he was today.

He met Wolfgang when he first came to the castle, and even spent quiet time with him, while they just listened to music in the background. Billy could tell that Wolfgang really enjoyed the music. His hands would move like he was playing the piano or violin at times, and at other times he would move his arms like he was conducting an orchestra.

"We can be caught up in the theatre of life, and feel powerful emotions that effect us physically. When we feel pain and guilt, or witness an unkind or violent act, either in our imagination or in real life we react. Our cells react. Our blood reacts. This is part of the passion of this life's play," Wolfgang began again.

"When fear and doubt creep in, as William has told you, we feel separated from our protection. We don't feel a mother's soothing touch or a father's comforting strength. We don't feel the presence of God's love that you've come to know in such a special way. We feel alone and lost and empty.

"And it's not enough that those lions of fear and doubt keep after us. And that we experience so much in life that brings us both sorrow and joy. But some other people, well-meaning or not, bring their emotions into our lives and push their particular limited views on us.

"If they have not known the exquisite joy of realizing fully who they are, and what this life can offer, they cannot teach us about it. They can only teach from pride and ego, from book information that tries to pass for genuine knowledge.

"The worst of them all are those who try to subdue and quiet us. The mediocre minds, those who live in a drab world, are troubled by those who would dare speak of something beyond the mundane. The mediocre are convinced that there is nothing more to life than what we can experience with our senses and our rational thinking.

"These types sometimes react loudly and violently. Others are more comfortable working insidiously, quietly undermining our efforts and our confidence. They work with the lions of fear and doubt. Instead of being a light in the world, expressing love and kindness, they put other people down and shout loud warnings. And they themselves don't really even understand why they do it. They have just learned this from other miserable and fearful people. It is so sad. But now you can make a difference, Billy.

"The other people here at the castle have talked to you about paintings and color as tools to defeat the lions grumbling. They are right. And, there's more. There's music. Music is marvelous and magical and glorious. Music stirs our heart and our soul, and resonates in our hearts, beyond words.

"When we really listen to music with all of our attention, we can enter into it. We can feel the resonance in the tonal vibrations. Music speaks to us of passion and of love, and of God's ever-present reality. It's in the magic of the instruments, in the composition designed by the maestro, and in the players whom he chooses to use to bring music's glorious message to the world.

"When we are longing to be attuned to God's reality, and when we are thirsty for a drink from his cup, music can bring us his soothing presence. There are times, Billy, when listening to music, that God speaks to our hearts so clearly that, even though there are no words, we know of his loving kindness and tender mercies toward us more clearly than any times in our lives. Music speaks of that most sacred of places we can experience as mortals.

"You've heard it before, Billy?" Wolfgang said loudly, after a long pause. "Listen once again."

After he said that, Wolfgang simply touched Billy on his left ear. Billy immediately heard the sweetest and most beautiful music.

As he listened he felt himself drift into that indescribable place of knowing God's immediate presence. He felt himself right back in the place he experienced after first entering into the light. He was savoring the moment when he heard another voice.

"Billy, you going to get out of the car?" Grampa asked.

At that, Billy snapped back. They had pulled into the driveway at Grampa's house. Billy was dazed and surprised. He had no recollection whatsoever of driving from the cemetery, or even getting in the car. His mind had been totally absorbed by his memories of being back at the castle, yet he had managed to drive home safely.

Billy thought to himself, "I wonder who is in charge of our driving when we do that?" He knew the answer.

Forgiveness

A ferocious dark memory
Billows over me without warning
A scarlet wave of emotion
Implodes my world
Drowns what were my dreams
Brings me to my knees
The wound oozes life
As I drift out to sea
And wash up on
A shore God forsaken
Mistaken for a corpse
Rotten flesh eaters
Encroach upon my art
Tear it apart mercilessly
And fly back to their caves
Clutching their weak worthless
Pitifully shallow commentaries
What others think
Will not shrink me to a toad
A fiery radiant angel
Cuts loose this heavy load
And forgiveness forgiveness
Calls me to live again
And walk a golden road

f o r g i v e n e s s

Chapter Eleven – Forgiveness

When Rachael got up the next morning, Billy and Grampa were already up and eating breakfast together. The house had an awfully somber feel to it. Billy and Grampa were eating cold cereal. The only sounds being made were the muffled crushing sounds of the cereal they were eating.

Rachael asked them if they wanted toast and juice or coffee. They were both kind of surprised to hear this from Rachael. Neither of them had known her to cook, not even toast. They nodded and gave each other a quick glance.

Rachael put on coffee, and while it was brewing, she made toast with butter and jam. Then she served Grampa a coffee, with toast, and she served Billy toast and orange juice. And she sat down with them at the table. They all sat silently while they finished their breakfast. Rachael started to pick up the dishes, and that brought another quick glance at each other from Billy and Grampa. Billy finally broke the stone silence in the house.

"How long are you staying around, Mom?"

"Oh, I was thinking of staying a couple of weeks. I don't know for sure. I was hoping that you and I could spend some time together."

"I'm moving back here to live with Grampa." Billy volunteered, not responding to his mother's plea for some time together. He knew they would spend time together.

So, Billy and Rachael carried on an uneasy chat, just kind of feeling each other out, while Grampa just got up and walked into the living room. He didn't even turn on the television. Now that may not sound like much of anything, but Grampa always had the television on in the living room. He could never stand silence. But now things were different. He would sit silently for hours on end, not even turning the light on when it got dark.

Over the next few days, Billy moved back home with Grampa. Rachael cooked simple meals, mostly from prepared and canned foods, and Grampa ate whatever she put in front of him. And he hardly spoke a word.

Rachael would find him asleep in his chair most mornings. She had tried to wake him up in the evening to try to get him to go to bed, but he'd just shake his head and wave her off. He also woke with such a start, every time she tried to wake him, that Rachael was happy to just let him sleep.

So, this whole somber mood hung in the air for days. Rachael would try to talk to Billy, but he always had something to do. Billy would try to talk to Grampa, but Grampa mostly shook his head one way or the other to respond, or just ignored what Billy had said, like he didn't hear him. It was awful, and it seemed like it would never be any different. But time has a way.

Billy came home one afternoon to find his mother's packed bags sitting in the kitchen next to the door. His mother hadn't said anything about leaving, but she had been around for about two weeks. When she came out of her room Billy asked her about her plans. She started to tell him that it was time for her to get back to Florida and all.

She was going along fine, pretty upbeat and all about how she had things to do and all. But in mid-sentence, she broke down. She slumped into a chair, put her hands in her face and sobbed in a way Billy had never seen. He was kind of surprised, but he was even more surprised by what she had to say.

"Billy, I've messed up my life so badly. I've hurt people so much, and I've been so selfish. I feel awful, almost all the time. Can you ever forgive me for being such a horrible mother? I know your father will never forgive me."

Billy couldn't believe his ears. It never occurred to him that his mother felt any remorse or guilt about leaving him and his father. He pretty much assumed that she didn't care about them and had her own life to live.

He hadn't really had much of a relationship with her at any time in his life, other than those few months after he came back from being missing. And then all she had done was keep him quiet so he wouldn't embarrass her, he thought.

But if you think Billy was surprised by her, well, he surprised her even more by what he said. It was just a simple phrase, heard by people every day, and said by people every day. Pretty ordinary little phrase.

"I love you, Mom."

It's funny how life can turn around so quickly. A quick lesson in life, a tune you hear, the smell in the air, or a simple phrase, a little clichéd bit of wisdom at the right time, call hit you like a thunderbolt. And your life is never the same again.

That's what happened this day. Rachael never went back to Florida. But let's not get ahead of the story. Rachael had never heard those words from Billy. She hadn't heard the words, "I love you", from anyone for a very long time. So they came like that thunderbolt. After a long pause, she finally told Billy that she loved him, too.

She stood up and hugged Billy tightly. He slowly put his arms around her and held on while she cried and cried. He thought she was still upset about Nana, and even though that was part of it, she was holding on to the words she never thought she would here. She felt like she didn't deserve to hear them. And that would lead to a long day's talk with her son.

A cab pulled into the driveway about then, and the driver tooted his horn a couple of times. Billy broke free and, without a word between them yet, he went out and told the cab driver that there had been a change of plans.

When Billy came back into the house, he looked at his mother with an adoration and respect that she couldn't begin to understand. She was the one stunned, now.

Billy explained to his mother about how he was so used to her coming and going, that when she left for good, all those years ago, it wasn't that big a deal for him. His father took it really hard, Billy told her, and that made him feel badly. But Billy was only eleven years old then, and it didn't feel the separation the same way his father felt it.

Rachael gave Billy the whole story. Seems she was in for a surprise herself when she got back to Florida. She had met this man a couple of years before, and they had moved in together a few months before Billy's disappearance. When Rachael came home for Billy, and then stayed away so long, he met someone else. Only he never told her.

As time went on, and Rachael and Ron got back together, this guy was telling Rachael how much he missed her and all. They'd stayed in touch. She would send him letters and they talked on the phone every so often.

It was kind of a bittersweet separation, and Rachael found that pretty romantic. Her letters got a little more passionate as she got caught up in the whole drama of this continuing long-distance love affair.

Well, when she got restless, she would conjure up this image of running back into his arms and returning to this wildly romantic scene. It was never really like that between them, but Rachael had a vivid fantasy life. That's where Billy inherited a lot of his creative imagination.

And so, one day, in the throws of this Hollywood imagery, Rachael packed up and left. That's when she wrote the farewell notes to Ron and Billy.

Problem was, this guy had hooked up with another woman, and she was living with him. He had just been stringing Rachael along. So when Rachael made her dramatic surprise entrance on the evening she arrived back in Florida, she walked into a nightmare.

Not only had she thoughtlessly and selfishly walked out on her family, with marriage plans ten days away. She had left her eleven year old son, again, and her mother and father, without a word of good-bye or explanation. She had expected to be able to wipe away all traces of that life, as she was swept up in the arms of her Florida love.

She was beaming as she so quietly opened the door that night, anticipating a return beam of delight. Instead, the feeling she got was more like a deer caught in the headlights of an oncoming car. Another woman was in her bed. And she wasn't alone.

Rachael felt that she had entered the twilight zone. She couldn't go home. She certainly couldn't stay there. She moved to another part of Florida, and lost contact with everyone. She pretty much lost contact with reality.

Her new friend came in a bottle. And she drifted into an alcoholic daze that lasted for years. Suicide crossed her mind time after time, but she never found the courage, or the weakness.

One day, on a weekend binge in Key West, she was spotted by a high school friend who recognized her. Rachael braved the encounter, and they exchanged addresses and phone numbers. They never called, but Rachael would get a letter every few months. That's how she connected back home, and how Billy eventually found out how to contact her in Florida.

As the day worn on, Rachael and Billy kind of bared their souls to each other. Oh, Billy had his own story. We'll get to that. Anyway, Rachael made an attempt to lighten up the conversation with what she thought would be a throwaway comment and chuckle.

"So, I guess that's how God paid me back."

"Mom, you got God all wrong," Billy fired back. "God doesn't punish, God forgives."

"I sure could use a lot of forgiveness, then." Rachael sighed.

As soon as Billy heard the word, "forgiveness", like so many times before, he thought about his time back at the castle.

Actually, this time it was quite different. He wasn't in a daydream like before. And he wasn't watching the events, from a detached view, as he did the last time. This time, the images and the words came directly from within him. They were his words and his images now. It was as if his time at the castle no longer felt distant and mysterious. And it also felt like the people he had met at the castle were now somehow a part of him, integrated into his thoughts and personality.

Oh, he remembered that it was Peter, the one who talked so fast, who told him about the painting, "Forgiveness", when Billy picked that painting. Peter said that it is something that God puts in your heart for you. And then he read the poem.

Billy found a pen and paper and wrote down the poem, which he then read to his mother.

Forgiveness

A ferocious dark memory
Billows over me without warning
A scarlet wave of emotion
Implodes my world
Drowns what were my dreams
Brings me to my knees
The wound oozes life
As I drift out to sea
And wash up on
A shore God forsaken
Mistaken for a corpse
Rotten flesh eaters
Encroach upon my art
Tear it apart mercilessly
And fly back to their caves
Clutching their weak worthless
Pitifully shallow commentaries
What others think
Will not shrink me to a toad
A fiery radiant angel
Cuts loose this heavy load
And forgiveness forgiveness
Calls me to live again
And walk a golden road

The expression that came over Rachael's face as she heard her young son read this poem is impossible to fully put into words. Her face and her features softened. Her prematurely lined eyes relaxed and a peacefulness she barely recognized came into her heart.

The first words she spoke were as much to give her time to adjust to this strangely unfamiliar and wonderful feeling, as they were from curiosity.

"A fiery radiant angel," she said. "I thought angels were all soft and gentle and played harp?"

"Some are soft and gentle, some are full of passion and energy," Billy said, matter-of-factly, as if this was a perfectly legitimate inquiry. "But there are fiery radiant angels, believe me."

Billy began to talk to his mother in such an enthusiastic and passionate way, that she soon forgot that this was her little boy, her baby, at one time. She was listening to someone speak to her, as if he were absolutely clear and sure of what he said. It was as if he had experienced the reality of this heavenly realm of which he spoke.

Billy told his mother about archangels. These are angels of great strength and power, he said. They are not the soft-spoken types that we stereotypically think of when we think of angels.

As a quick aside, he mentioned that neither are the saints and sages from all the religions and spiritual paths, the ever humble and gentle souls we have come to image them being.

"Jesus wasn't facilitating a support group, he was trying to break through the myth and dulled and ignorant minds of the day, and tell his people about a God of love and caring and kindness that he knew personally.

And when he needed to, believe me, he could be tough. There's a story about him throwing tables over when he saw merchants at the temple. He could be fiery.

"Krishna told Arjuna of fierce battles of the mind. Even some of gentle Buddha's disciples have been known to whack aspirants with a stick to snap them out of a dazed consciousness and into another more enlightened one. There are fiery radiant angels, mom," Billy reiterated.

"There is an enemy, an opposite, a darkness, whatever you want to call it, that comes against our right and privilege to enjoy life to the fullest. We were created to be a light and a manifestation of love, not to live in fear and doubt, and all that fear and doubt creates in our mind.

"I was taught to think of the enemies of our peace of mind and joy in this life, as lions. They are the lions of fear and doubt. They are blatant liars. If we listen to them, they will try to convince us that we are not worthy of forgiveness. They focus on the wrong we've done. They are even clever enough to quote scripture out of context to convince us that we are sinful by nature.

"That is one of the most joy robbing, damaging and discouraging pieces of teaching that parrots in the pulpit spit out.."

Here, Rachael had to interrupt Billy, because she didn't know what he meant. So he took time to explain that, as many truly enlightened spiritual teachers tell us, there are "false teachers" who teach only what they have been told by other blind and false teachers.

Billy went on to tell his mother that we are all good and perfect by nature. He said that it is only the false teachings, and the lions of doubt and fear that these false teachings activate, that dulls our mind and creates darkness where the sun is meant to shine. The sun is meant to shine in our hearts, in our hearts, Billy repeated several times to make his point.

This darkness will keep us from realizing that we will always be forgiven for anything and everything we have done, as soon as we look to our hearts and allow that sun to rise, that light to re-appear.

It is a light that brings the knowledge of our inherent goodness, regardless of what we have done in darkness. And when we feel and see that spark of goodness, we know that we are a spark of God's own fire, and a divinity exists within everyone.

When that light shines, when we hear music that resonates in our hearts, when we see colors that appear to us with a magical glow – in the world, in paintings, in someone's funny hat, we return to the awareness of that goodness. And that goodness comes with kindness and compassion and love for all of mankind, and all of creation. We can step into a place of perfection.

When we listen to fear and doubt, we not only can find ourselves in darkness, with all sorts of dark thoughts about ourselves, we can begin to project these thoughts on others. This is where unforgiveness comes from.

And so Billy came to the title of the poem and the issue of forgiveness. He told his mother that the toughest person in the world to forgive is ourselves. Forgiving others can be hard, but forgiving ourselves is really tougher.

Because as we dredge up those things that we did that we feel guilty and ashamed of, we come close to those lions of fear and doubt and they begin to chatter. Their chatter can become almost constant, and that inner voice keeps condemning us and condemning us.

In those moments when we are feeling really good about ourselves and about our place in the world, is a time when we can soften and forgive everyone who has ever hurt us in any way.

We might even recognize that we may have had a part in creating the problem. As we think of the person we are still mad at, or are not willing to forgive, our thoughts go to them, and the lions are not as able to get our attention so easily.

But when it comes to ourselves, a ferocious dark memory can bring us to our knees. We can hear the voices of our accusers and the gossipers, and their judgmental appraisals of our behavior. The lions are wonderful mimics of other people's voices. If we are not able break out of our remorse, we can begin to be so concerned with what other people think that this concern becomes the god we serve.

"Don't be concerned with what other people think, Mom. Know that God is a God of forgiveness and love," Billy preached with passion, as he spoke to his mother. And then it came out.

"Billy, I told God that I hated him! How can I be forgiven for that?" Rachael blurted.

Billy laughed, and that really upset her. But Billy continued to assure her that God is not like some hateful schoolgirl or boy who gets so mad that they never want to speak to you again. God knows about the lions of fear and doubt.

God's bigger than that. God is bigger than our bad mood, crazy ideas and ego concepts. He's bigger than religion or culture. We can't put God in a box. God is available to every living person, probably every living thing. We do not own God. God is our creator. And God loves us, with a love that is unconditional. We put the conditions on it.

We are taught that God judges us, but he does not! God allows us to take whatever path we choose in life. And whenever it occurs to us that we have taken the wrong path, and we turn to look for help, God is always right there. And as a great teacher said, 'It is God's great pleasure to present us the kingdom".

God wants us happy and free of fear and doubt. That's what turning to God does, it frees us of fear and doubt, and allows his tender mercies and radiant beam of light to bring our hearts alive and full of joy.

When that happens, we get zero mileage on our conscience complete forgiveness felt from within, and we completely forgive everyone who has ever offended us. We again become radiant lights of love and purity that we were as newborn babes.

We feel love and kindness and compassion for all. That is God's character, and it becomes our character when the sun rises every day. We just have to bask in God's love, God's sunrise, every day.

As we do everything becomes fresh and new again, including us. And when we learn how to stop listening to those lions of fear and doubt and look for the light, we live in paradise – right here on earth.

That's the way it was meant to be. And when we wander away as we all do, we have a helper, a light to guide us back. That's the holy spirit, the inner guidance, the inner light that all the great masters speak of in their teachings.

"Your father will never forgive me," Rachael countered, still holding on to the old fears and doubts that had been her companion for so long. She and Billy would have many, many talks before that would change for good.

"He will as soon as he forgives himself," Billy said. Rachael went back to her room and unpacked. She knew that she and Billy had a lot more to talk about.

Grampa was still sitting quietly in the silence of the living room. He had heard pieces of what Billy had said, especially when Billy became passionate and loud as he talked to his mother. Grampa was a bit unnerved. He would talk to Billy later. Billy went up to his room and unpacked his paints.

Now Billy hadn't painted much of anything for quite a few years. He had painted and sold a few pieces of quiet landscapes and scenes from the lake. But they had no passion in them. Today would prove to be very different.

Instead of drawing a scene in pencil and then carefully filling in the colors, as was his usual approach, Billy attacked the canvas! He almost threw paint at it. His brushstrokes were quick and fluid and sweeping. His color choices were bold and bright. The painting he had seen back at the castle, the painting entitled, "Forgiveness", appeared as if by magic on the easel in front of him.

Billy was so entranced by the fact that he was painting so passionately that it never even entered his mind that he was trying to recreate any other painting. He was just enjoying the passion of the moment and the swift movement of his hands and eyes, and the brush. But there it was, polished and precisely the way he had seen it before.

When he recognized the painting, it froze him on the spot, much in the way he froze under the ice so long ago. And then it happened.

Billy felt himself pulled into the painting, like you see in a special effects movie. As he passed by the deep blue and green colors and into the red and then gold, he found himself once again on the mountain, looking at a figure with a flowing, glowing robe. And once again as he looked down a pathway he saw the white light, and just as before, he was in that special place of God's presence.

He could feel the waves of pure love wash over him. The joy was almost more than he could bear, but at the same time he never wanted to leave this place of profound and perfect peace of mind. Checkered light began to flicker around him. He felt as if he were surrounded by angels.

And then, in a matter of seconds, it was over. Billy was back in front of his painting. But it wasn't over. Everything he experienced came back with him. He thought he would break out laughing, but he just smiled this broad smile from ear to ear, and he glowed with a glow that filled the room.

As he looked back at the painting and realized once more that he had finally created one of the paintings from his room at the castle, he was filled with anticipation. He knew what was to come.

Anticipation

Flames from some
Mysterious torch
Blazed and beckoned
A reddish ochre tongue
Conspired to take my life
Lava flows crept into my brain
A painful insane invitation
Arrived unannounced uninvited
Obliterated my senses
And told me I must go
Into the hellish dark night
Leaving no explanation
Never never to come back
Dead reckoning
Guided me
Chided me
About a wretched past
Until at last
The indigo torch
Grazed my temple
And removed the haze
Light the way home
Said the ancient of days
Paint your way home

a n t i c i p a t i o n

Chapter Twelve – Anticipation

Billy didn't even remember getting into bed and falling asleep that night. His mind was filled with visions of the twelve paintings. He reviewed them all in his inner vision, over and over. With the vision of each painting came the words of the lessons, and the person who taught them. And there was William after each lesson talking to Billy about the lions.

In a way, he understood so much more now. But in another way, he felt as if he already knew everything he was taught, even then. That brief experience in the presence of God, before Billy came to the castle, had given him a wisdom beyond words, and certainly beyond his years.

He was only ten years old when he fell through the ice and into another reality. Now he was twenty-three. At ten he had heard the words the way any ten year old would here them.

As he heard them again, he was hearing them as a twenty-three year old. He was still very young, by any standard, but he had experienced life in many ways that some people never know.

He could hear William so clearly. He could see those kind and gentle eyes peering out from behind that long dark hair that would fall in front of his face from time to time.

"The lions of fear and doubt will stalk you, all of your life, Billy. They will look for opportunities to point out a wrong that you or someone else has done. As soon as you entertain that idea, they will step up the chatter.

"As you rehearse your view of something you see as wrong, in your mind, the lions will applaud and encourage the object of your judgment of right and wrong.

"And it doesn't matter if you are judging a person's behavior or the quality of a pair of shoes you are considering buying. They will find the flaw and point it out to you, if you listen to them. They are always ready to present their negative point of view.

"Once you listen, fear and doubt are back in your mind. And they will take control for as long as you allow them to dictate the course of your life.

"This will happen to you as life goes on, Billy. Don't think it won't. That is part of life, and part of how we grow to great strength and wisdom. With each victory over the intrusion from the lions, we become stronger and more solid. But they will never give up, entirely. And it would be a great mistake to think that you have conquered them once and for all.

"I'm not talking about fearing them. I'm talking about keeping your focus, as you go through life. There's so much to complain about, and so much misery and pain in the world that it is easy to get discouraged and lose your way.

"The lions love to point this out and ridicule anyone who says that life can be full of joy. They tell us to look at the pain and suffering. And, of course, they blame God or Mother Nature, or some higher power for the pain and suffering. But it isn't God who causes the pain and suffering, it is most often how people treat each other.

"We have abundance on this earth, yet there is hunger and starvation. That's not God's doing. He created the abundance. It's mankind's doing, or actually man's unkind doing. Even tragic accidents and crashes are man's doing. But the lions will prey on people's mind and ask them how God could let something happen.

"What are we to do then, Billy? How can we enjoy life to the fullest?' William answered his own questions.

"By keeping our minds open to God's love, and leaving things we have no way of understanding in God's hands. It takes an experience of God's love to enable us to understand this fully and do this as a way of life. And those who have been touched by God's love in a real and experiential way, know this.

"The people who have come to understand that there is a power or energy that is greater than our individual consciousness are the ones who are called to show this to other people.

"It is an experience of God's love. You are one of these people who will bring God's love to others, when the time is right. You will understand this much more clearly as you mature.

"Just as the lions will never leave you alone entirely, what has happened to you will never leave you. The meaning of your experience will continue to unfold ever new meaning to you all of your life.

"What has happened to you is much stronger than the lions and will defeat them at every turn. You will always have a choice. You can listen to the lions or you can listen to your heart. Your heart contains clear wisdom, and will show you clearly the right path to choose in any instance, in any circumstance. When you are attuned to your heart wisdom, all of you choices are perfect and your life and your heart are filled with joy.

"When you heart is filled with joy, you glow. And the world sees this glow. When you are influenced by fear and doubt your glow dims. You came here to learn these lessons.

"You have been given a gift of wisdom and knowledge. Take this gift to all you meet. Show God's character of love and kindness in your every thought and every action, as best you can. This is what the great teachers and masters of spiritual truth are able to do. This is what they bring to the world. That is the purpose of their lives.

" This is a very easy thing to do, a natural thing to do. But it is also a very narrow path to walk. There are many other paths that the lions, and those whom they have influenced, will try to lead you down.

"The most insidious thing they do is lead you down a path of pain and misery, and then blame you for what has happened. You made a wrong choice or several wrong choices. You listened to them, so they hold you accountable. And you will hold yourself accountable.

"The difference is that as soon as you realize that you have made a wrong choice, and sometimes this can take years, you can return to the path of light and wisdom immediately. From that moment, it will be possible for every action you take will be from the heart of wisdom.

"We are completely restored and forgiven every time we return to the way of the heart. It happens immediately, Billy. God's love will never leave you.

"But the lions do not give up that easily. They will tell you that God is displeased with you, or that God doesn't love you because of what you did or didn't do. They will chatter away that you have blown your chance with God.

"This is the most insidious lie. You can never blow your chance with God. God will always forgive you and welcome you back into this kingdom, over and over and over, as long as you live. It happens the moment you turn to seek God's presence and guidance.

nstantly. Always."

Billy chuckled to himself to remember how fired up William was this time. It was right after Peter talked to him about the painting and poem entitled, "Forgiveness".

As he thought back to this time, Billy was half asleep, half awake. It occurred to him that he had said almost exactly what Peter had said to him about the painting and poem to him. He wasn't aware of it at the time, but he had spoken to his mother, earlier that day, very much in the way Peter had spoken to him years ago.

Billy had just started talking to his mother about forgiveness, without thinking back to the time with Peter. Billy hadn't realized it, at the time, but he talked to his mother using the same feeling and conviction that he had seen in Peter.

"Wow," Billy said out loud as he realized what had happened. He was painting the paintings, talking the talk. "Talking the talk, walking the walk," he thought to himself.

As Billy lay in bed that morning, he almost expected to hear Nana's voice calling him to breakfast. As a wave of sadness washed over him, he shook it off and recalled those moments of joy and delight with his grandmother.

He thought of that flash of seeing her holding a piece of apple pie and cold milk at the castle. He chose to dwell on those positive images for a few seconds, and he felt his heart lighten.

Getting dressed, Billy was hit with another wave of emotion. This one was a wave of excitement that built to exhilaration. He was thinking about how he now felt so confident in his ability to paint the paintings. And he thought about how much more meaning the stories of the paintings now held for him now. It was happening as William had told him that it would. The flower was beginning to come into fuller blossom.

In the next moment, he realized clearly that it was God coming through him, God's inspiration, that was allowing him to create the paintings. He wondered why he had not been able to do this earlier. Remember, he had thought that he would be able to paint the paintings back when he was ten. But he couldn't. He heard William's voice respond to his questioning thought.

"We teach what we most need to learn, Billy. It's a delight, the way it sometimes works. When we are struggling to understand something, trying to find some reason for our despair or confusion, or feeling out of touch with God's love for us, we'll often bump into someone else who's going through the same thing.

"The details may be different, but the lesson they need to be reminded of is very much the same. When you spoke to your mother about forgiveness, you needed to hear that as well. When you told her that your father would be able to forgive her when he forgave himself, you needed to hear that, too.

"Do you see, Billy? When we are kind and compassionate and willing to help others, we are the ones who receive help as well. Being of service to someone else, helping someone else through a difficult time does incredibly good things for our own heart and our own sense of who we are.

"Like so many things you've heard, this needs to be experienced to be fully understood. People who set out to do good deeds out of a sense of obligation may feel good about what they do, but those who help others from the goodness of their hearts, stir up that very goodness. And their own spirits are lifted in the process of helping someone else.

"They experience a joy much like what you felt when you

came to your room after talking with your mother. There's a joy in being of service to others. And you've experienced it.

"Now you are filled with anticipation about the future and have come to realize your purpose in life. So listen to what you told your mother. Forgive yourself for all of the things you've done that make you feel guilty. You will now realize more clearly and completely than before, that God is a God of forgiveness. Go on with a new life, once again. Paint your way home, Billy."

Well, those last few words that came to Billy just jolted him. He sat back down on his bed, and he saw another painting and poem. It was like they were right in the room with him, right in front of his eyes.

He had heard the words and seen the painting before, but now it felt to him like he was creating them for the first time.

Anticipation

Flames from some
Mysterious torch
Blazed and beckoned
A reddish ochre tongue
Conspired to take my life
Lava flows crept into my brain
A painful insane invitation
Arrived unannounced uninvited
Obliterated my senses
And told me I must go
Into the hellish dark night
Leaving no explanation

Never never to come back
Dead reckoning
Guided me
Chided me
About a wretched past
Until at last
The indigo torch
Grazed my temple
And removed the haze
Light the way home
Said the ancient of days
Paint your way home

The words were there, the painting clearly in his mind, and he could hear Cynthia's soft and soothing voice reading the poem to him. As Billy anticipated a return trip to the castle, he was filled with a strange feeling of coming home, again. Only this time he didn't go to the castle, where his thoughts and memories so often took him. He remained in his room at Nana's. And Cynthia came to him.

She looked exactly the way he remembered her from so many years ago. She was a woman of substantial size, with flawless skin, dimples when she smiled – which was most of the time, and the softest blue eyes you've ever seen.

The colors she usually wore were as soft as her graceful manner and movement; pastels and creamy whites, with a splash of bright red or green somewhere. The splash of color could be a flower in her hair or behind her ear, or a bracelet or shoes. But it was always there, like a focal point. It was like an unlikely exclamation point at the end of a softly spoken sentence.

She commanded attention when she spoke. Not from a boomng voice, but from a voice so soft and calm that you had to pay attention to hear what she was saying. That, and the fact that she touched you when she spoke.

She would ever so gently lay her hand on your arm, with maybe just one or two fingers barely making contact. And she said, "Oh", a lot. All this had a way of mesmerizing Billy.

"Oh, Billy. You've come to anticipation" Cynthia began. "This is the beginning of your return home."

Those words rang like a bell in Billy's ears. He had heard them exactly that way back at the castle, way back when he was there earlier. But now he was home, back at his home. And Cynthia had come to him.

"Heaven is right here on earth," Billy thought to himself. Or rather, the thought came to him. He was kind of surprised at this thought and not really clear about why it came to him at this particular moment. He was about to find out, as Cynthia's soft and compelling voice continued.

"We come into this life as babies, fresh and brand new to life. We are cared for and fed and protected. We see smiling, cooing faces. So naturally we come to see life as a beautiful and benevolent experience. We are surrounded by tenderness and love. As very young children, we are awed by the sights and sounds and smells, taste and touch of everything we see. A bug can be an adventure.

"In the midst of this, as very young children, we remember, in a way without words, that we came out of heaven. We begin to glow and everyone who sees us feels that glow. A young child who comes into a room can melt everyone in the room with her glow and sparkle. This is our time of first experiencing heaven on earth.

"But then, in just a few months or years, we begin to hear and see things that are not nice. We see people crying. We hear people hollering. We are told that we are "bad" because of something we did, like we spilled a glass of milk. Someone yanks us by the arm so strongly that it hurts. We begin to notice pain, physically and emotionally.

"This wonderfully benevolent place that we were so delighted to be a part of, is suddenly filled with warnings. Darkness that was peaceful and quiet now becomes frightening. Slowly, but steadily, our glow dims. Our memory fades, and we feel lost and separated from the joy and peace and love we once knew as a way of life.

"Oh, we feel it every so often. But not for long. A voice of fear and doubt creeps in. A stern voice of discipline booms in. We are told of demons and devils and things that will hurt us. The list of what is wrong and what is right grows longer and longer. And every time we do something that we have been told is wrong, a voice inside chides us, reminds us, that have done something wrong.

"We try to blot out the memory and silence the inner voice. We busy ourselves with life. The memory of where we came from, the heaven that we can experience here on earth, and the heaven we will return to after our time on earth is done, is all forgotten.

"Now we fear the hellish dark night. We feel lost and afraid, and we have been told, in the words and actions of other lost and afraid people, that we are bad and worthless.

"We worry that we will be found out. We imagine that some strange creature will attack us and devour us. We fear for our lives. We accept that we are in a hostile and dangerous place.

"The terrible false teachers, the parrots that Jonathan spoke about, the lions of fear and doubt that William has taught you about, begin to rule our lives. And our lives, the lives of most people, become what one writer named, Henry David Thoreau, called, 'lives of quiet desperation.'

"But, Billy, oh, Billy, many people, and you are one of them are touched by God in such a way that they are consciously brought back the magic of that time as a child. They return to that sense of the world being a beautiful and benevolent place. They come back into the arms of God. And their lives are changed forever.

"You came to it very young, and you needed some life experiences to more fully understand just how precious a gift you have received. You have known, since you were ten years old, that you are special and that something special is required of you.

"Oh, and you know something else, Billy? Everyone has a little voice inside that tells them that they are special, too. And everyone knows, even if they have buried that voice deep, deep inside, that something special is required of them, too.

"The difference for you came from the time you fell through the ice. You came to the castle. Now, you are among the many people who are touched by God's love in their lives, and have a sure knowledge of the reality of God.

"You have been immersed in God's love, so immersed that you will never again feel entirely separated from God. Oh, that's an interesting word, immersed.

"You have this knowledge, this experience, and you have heard the voice, the urging within, to share this knowledge. You are meant to speak of it. You cannot keep the voice quiet for very long, can you, Billy? It is too sweet to be denied.

"Your mother and your father were afraid of it. Your grandfather freaked out about it. But your grandmother didn't want you to keep quiet about it. She knew you had something special to share.

"And now, Billy. It is your time. You have seen pain and fear and doubt. You have experienced guilt and despair yourself. But nothing has erased the experience of God's reality in your life, has it, Billy? Oh, no. That will never happen.

"So paint, Billy, and write the poems. They will all come back clearly to you now. Just remember that we teach most what we need to learn. As you show the paintings and poems to your father and your grandfather, and as you talk to them about what they need to hear, you will grow in wisdom and clarity.

"You will increase your understanding. Keep a journal, Billy. Write down your experiences. Tell others. Tell everyone who will listen. Paint the paintings. Paint your way home."

That was all she said, and in a blink, Cynthia was gone.

Well, if Billy had happily anticipated the upcoming day before this visit from Cynthia, and had entertained a lively vision of what was to come, this put him into orbit. Joy begins to describe it, but it was much more. Much more.

Billy felt a sense of wellbeing and purpose in life, the depths of which he had never experienced. He was yet to encounter some of the obstacles still in his way, and in a way he knew that, too. But his confidence in what he knew and what he had to say about his experiences grew even stronger in those few minutes.

Actually, that confidence had been growing ever so gradually for years and years. But now he was freer than ever before. He was now free to be exactly whom he knew himself to be, and to express exactly what he knew to be true in life.

He knew exactly what the poem, the painting, and the words Cynthia used meant. He was ready to paint his way home. And he knew that he could now create the paintings, or rather that the paintings would be created at the end of his brush. That was more the way he thought about it.

What he did not anticipate was how clearly the words William had spoken to him so many years ago would come back to him in the next few weeks and months. William told him how mean and close-

minded some people can be when they have been influenced by the
ions of fear and doubt all their lives.

But Billy had no way to know how ferociously some people
will fight back at anything or anyone who presumes to offer them a
way to find their way back to love and joy and peace of mind.

People who have been so hurt by life that they feel complete-
y defeated often become bitter and closed off from any real emotions
other than fear and doubt. They know only deep, deep anger at what
they conceive to be the cause of their pain.

Often it is their imagination that causes them the most dis-
tress. They hear the lies of the internal chatter, echoing the words of
the lions, and they become convinced that there are no satisfactory
answers to their questions, nor is there any relief for their pain.

"You can bring them the answer, Billy. You know that God's
love is the answer. A knowledge of God's love for them will change
their hearts. And God's love contains all the answers. God answers in
ways that man's mind cannot conceive," William had said to Billy
many times, he remembered.

Billy began to recall much of what William and the other people at the castle had told him. But once again, the thoughts and words
seemed to be his own, rather than something he was being told by
someone else. His thoughts continued.

Many people feel abandoned by God, at times in their lives,
because in a time of need they found no help. People, not God, abandoned them. Others feel that life did not give them a fair shake. They
were born into poverty or a household of violence and confusion.

Some people come out of these circumstances to do great
things in life, while others from the same environment feel empty and
lost most of their lives. There are even people who really have so much

in life to be grateful for, but have given in to constant complaining and self-pity to the point where they are unhappy with almost every moment of their life. And they deeply resent the happiness that they see in others.

At the extreme, they scream at any intrusion into their private hell. They fear only more hurt and pain will come if they allow new information or point of view into their thinking. The stubbornly refuse to release their hold on reality as they see it.

They have shut off their emotions, and have walled themselves in for protection from any more pain. What they don't realize is that they have also walled themselves off from any love coming in. These walls can be awfully tough to break through. But unconditional love can do it. Billy would find that out.

These words and many more would come to Billy over the next few weeks and months as he painted the paintings he knew so well. He painted, "Transformation, Silence, Devotion, Elation, and Passion." And his devotion, elation and passion grew. And the clarity of his vision returned.

Because Billy was in such balanced harmony with life and with his connection to God, he began to notice any small event or exchange between people that reflected that harmony.

A kind deed would bring a kind word from Billy. It kind of melted people when Billy would acknowledge their thoughtful gesture. Billy loved to see the look on people's face when he would compliment them on what he had seen them do. It could be something as simple as someone smiling at someone else as they passed by.

Billy would say things to them like, "How wonderful of you to smile at that scruffy old man, and bring a little light into his life. What a wonderful person you must be."

Billy saw so much goodness and caring in people. He began to hear of God's love for us in every song he would hear on his radio. He saw mercy and grace and God's light shine through so many works of art.

He saw God's love acknowledging God's love in every person with whom he made eye contact. He spoke of experiencing heaven right here on earth. His heart was so full of joy, his words just bubbled when he spoke.

But, of course, as happens to anyone who is bold enough to openly declare that they "know" of a loving God, some of those who do not know, and insist that no one can know, come strongly against them.

Billy often heard harsh rejection of his words. His paintings were ridiculed in a newspaper article, and he was even called insane by a particularly loud and belligerent man on the street one day.

As this man cursed and shouted obscenities, his whole appearance started to change right before Billy's eyes. The man turned into a large black crow. His eyes became green and iridescent. The wind began to blow, and Billy kind of wondered if the devil himself hadn't made an appearance.

This scene unnerved Billy a bit, until he heard a familiar booming laugh. It was Jim.

Sunrise At Two Lions

The Breeze

Midnight black crows
You pretenders
To a throne
You do not own
There is no magic
In your caustic words
Mean and spiteful
Frightful flightful birds
Green and iridescent
Flashing hatefulness
Sick with evil intent
Meant to impale
My attempts
To break free
Squawk your talk
Will not belittle me
Criticize and analyze
All you please
Thanks to you
Who would unto
A mystic sojourn
I will earn the victory
I will come to sea
And ride the colors
Of the breeze

t h e   b r e e z e

Chapter Thirteen – The Breeze

Billy heard Jim's laugh as clearly as if Jim had been standing right beside him. And immediately, the time with Jim, the painting that Jim talked about, and the poem that went with it all came rushing into Billy's awareness.

As soon as that happened, the big black crow returned to the shape of the small, but loud and belligerent man standing in front of Billy. Billy must have smiled sweetly or something, because the man went silent, looked a little dazed, then turned and walked away without another word.

Now, as you well know by now, William spent a lot of time with Billy teaching him about all of the tricks and tomfoolery of the lions, but this guy, Jim, was different.

He talked about the lions, too. But mostly he talked about people Billy would meet who would claim to know much more than Billy. Jim talked about people who would authoritatively insist that Billy couldn't know what he knew, and that it all was a young boy's fantasy and need for attention, and all that pseudo-intellectual stuff. That's what Jim called it.

Jim was a big, barrel-chested man with a beard that made him look even bigger. If you didn't know him, or you didn't take time to look a little closer, you could mistake him for a big bully. But if you took a second to catch the look in his eyes and the little smirk in his smile, you could see that he was a softhearted teddy bear.

Of course, you also know by now that Jim was one of the twelve people that Billy met at the castle. One of the very vivid memories Billy had of Jim was how everyone who even came close to Jim to talk to him or listen to him, always gave him a big hug.

Billy often thought that everyone who knew Jim must really love him. And Billy loved the way that Jim's booming laugh would occasionally ring all through the big house that Billy always thought of as a castle.

But there was another side to Jim, and Billy had witnessed that a few times, too. It seemed to show mostly when Jim was somewhere near the lions. As much as his laugh boomed, it was nothing compared to when he shouted. Billy thought he saw the stone lions even tremble a time or two.

Billy was never quite sure what had upset Jim. Maybe he was learning about the lions, too, Billy thought at those moments. Maybe the lions were trying to create fear and doubt in Jim. As this thought hit Billy, on the street that day, he kind of reeled back on his heels. A flood of possibilities hit him.

He had thought, maybe not consciously or in exactly that way, but he had thought that he was the only one at the castle who had come there to be taught about the lions and the paintings.

Maybe everyone was there for this reason. They could have all been there to learn something, in the way they needed to learn it. William had said to him many times that we teach most what we need to learn.

Anyway, Billy thought about that possibility as he got in his car and started to drive on home. On the way, he chuckled to himself s the recalled the man who changed into a crow, and how he heard im laugh. Then he went into that place we go when we keep driving out we don't remember any of it. Billy went back to the castle, once more. This time he went way back to when he was only ten years old.

"*Don't let that one knock you over*, there, Billy. You couldn't weigh more than sixty pounds soaking wet. Oops, sorry about that soaking-wet crack." boomed this voice. It was Jim, looking over Billy's shoulder as he stared at the painting. "It's called, 'The Breeze'. Let me tell you about it."

The Breeze

Midnight Black crows
You pretenders
To a throne
You do not own
There is no magic
In your caustic words
Mean and spiteful
Frightful flightful birds
Green and iridescent
Flashing hatefulness
Sick with slick intent
Meant to impale
My attempts
To break free
Your caws
Will not belittle me
Squawk your talk

Criticize and analyze
All you please
You who would undo
A mystic sojourn
I will earn the victory
I will come to sea
And ride the colors
Of the breeze

"This is about people who think they know it all, but really don't know nothing," Jim began. As you'll see and hear, Jim was not about pretense or culture or politically correct anything. Jim was Jim, take him or leave him. Just don't irritate him, if you can't handle an outburst back. Jim was a bear. Now, he was a gentle bear, but a bear nonetheless.

"When you go home, Billy, some people are going to want to keep you quiet. Your mother may be embarrassed by what you say. She's afraid of what other people will think, and she's afraid that God is mad at her. I know that's kind of silly, knowing what you know now, but she is convinced that she is not worthy to be welcomed by God.

"Your father and your grandfather have this pubic façade about how down-to-earth and practical they are in their approach to life. To even think about God makes them shudder. They think it's all foolishness. So they won't want to hear about anything to do with God at all.

"Course, they need to hear about it about as much as anybody, because they are so afraid of death that it scares them to even hear the word, 'God'. It's kind of weird, but they would like to believe. They are just scared to believe, in a way. You'll see.

"Now your grandmother, she's all right. She knows, in her

182

eart, that there is something going on in this life beyond our senses nd our intellect. She believes in God. She believes in a kind of benev- ·lent and informative energy. You know, like when she reads tealeaves.

"These are the people, the people who are in your family, vhom you will talk to the most about what you have experienced and vhat you are learning here. It will take some time, but they will listen o you and they will come to know the truth that you know, in their vay.

"When you're older, you'll have a chance to tell a lot of peo- ›le, and you'll have an effect upon a lot of lives. But that's for later.

"William's talked to you about the lions, so I don't have to talk bout that. You ever notice how much William repeats himself? Man! \nyway, I want to talk to you about people who will really freak out .bout the story you will tell.

"First of all, you will have been gone a long time, by the time ·ou get back home. And people are going to want a rational explana- ion. They're not going to get one. Then when you start to tell your tory of coming into God's presence, and coming to the castle, you'll ose a lot of them. And you will probably stop talking about this vhole episode for a time.

"But the day will come when you will pick up and continue ›n the journey that is to be your life's purpose. It will take some pow- :rful motivation and some difficult life lessons to give you the courage .nd energy to tell your story, no matter what. But the day will come.

"When you do finally decide, when you step up strongly and ›assionately, knowing that you will devote the rest of your life to shar- ng this knowledge of God's love, there will be no turning back. A ïerce wind will begin to blow against you, Billy. A wind like you've 1ever known will come up. The lions will mount an attack more insis- :ent and convincing then ever before.

"They will remind you of every mistake you've ever made, every unkind word you've ever said, or that was said to you. They will insist over and over that you are mistaken about what you want to do.

"They will tell you that you are being foolish and self-centered, that no one will believe you. And, of course, they will tell you that you have blown your chance with God. They will tell you that God does not love you, and that the awful things you did prove that you do not sincerely want to serve God.

"But that's not the worst of it, Billy. The most fierce attack, the most violent of winds, will come from the most unlikely places. They will come from people who profess to know more than you, people who will insist that you are a phony and a storyteller living a fantasy life.

"These pretenders will warn others of the dangers of your teachings and your stories. I know it's hard to imagine that people need to be warned about someone talking about a God of love and kindness who wants them to have a life full of joy.

"Some people will be so upset by what you say that they will literally want to kill you, Billy. I know that sounds ridiculous, but believe you me, it has happened before.

"So, when the time comes that you begin to see clearly that what has happened to you here will determine the course of your life, you will begin to remember what I am saying to you now.

"The breeze will begin to blow. Let it strengthen your resolve. Let it bring you back fully to the reality of God's love and your time in God's presence.

"So many people are waiting to hear this, Billy. Don't let the blind and angry belittlers stop you. Let them analyze and criticize all they please. Remember what you have been told so many times. Experience is never at the mercy of argument. Remember what you ave experienced."

As Billy heard these last few words from Jim, "Remember what you have experienced," a sense of peace and tranquility came over him. He watched the light turn green and as he stepped on the gas, he realized that he was truly on his way home.

It took Billy just two days to complete the paintings of Anticipation and The Breeze. He watched these paintings appear before his eyes exactly and precisely the way he remembered them from before.

The choice and blend of colors, and the flow of the paint from his brush to the canvas on his easel all felt like it was all taking place effortlessly.

As Billy looked at the paintings, he felt his resolve grow. The more he looked at his paintings, now numbering a total of eight paintings, the more he knew that nothing on earth would keep him from telling about God's love. He would tell about it in his paintings and in the words that he would speak.

The streak of white light in the painting, The Breeze, looked one moment like the crest of a wave, then in another moment like the light of God that he knew so well. The light that invited him into that most beautiful place he knew so well, God's very presence. That incredibly comforting, peaceful, freeing, dancing, loving, laughing, rejoicing place in his heart responded to this painting.

The pink and peach horizon spoke to him of his earlier transformation. The dark blues and stormy colors of the sea held no threat for him. In fact, they brought him in touch with a deep inner courage, a bravery that felt brand new to him.

He loved the way this felt, and he began to spend several minutes a day sitting on the edge of his bed, looking at this painting that somehow came from his mind, and hand, and brush. It all just delighted him.

He would sit at night with his lampshade tipped to cast the light on this painting. He would play music and dance, all by himself in his room.

"I choose to dance, unafraid," he said out loud one evening. It was like that sentence came out of his mouth without thought, and he heard it when he first spoke it. He repeated in over and over, in his mind. He liked the sound and meaning of that.

Billy was coming to trust in himself, to know himself. He was coming home. He was painting his way home. And in the telling of his connection to God, he was gaining strength and resolve everyday.

One evening, in the midst of his dancing, unafraid, he felt so inspired and joyful and free that he raised his arms up high and shouted out the word, freedom.

This would catapult him into his next painting and into a time with his family unlike any time any of them ever expected. Billy would talk to them of their past and their future. The theme would come from his next painting.

Freedom

Poison tipped
white lies
Fly Swiftly
Their whispered hissings
Silently decry
My burgundy dark deeds
These arrows drunk
With excessive wine
Still easily find
Their mark
Sharp merciless fangs
Drag me to the ground
Biting wounding louts
Have found me out
Pleading for release
I am left bleeding
Deep blue eons of time
Confine me find me
In a beggar's grip
But then I am delivered
Before the queen of kindness
Who melts my chains
Lays claim to my sanity
And grants my
Freedom

f r e e d o m

Chapter Fourteen – Freedom

*T*he painting came first this time. When Billy shouted the word, freedom, that evening, the image came so vividly that it stopped him in his dancing tracks. He dove into the painting immediately, and like all the others, he simply watched it take shape and color on the fresh canvas that he now kept handy on the easel in his room.

"Freedom", the finished painting, seemed to Billy to be ready to fly. And it cried to make itself known to his grandfather even before it had dried. Billy marched downstairs with the painting, and presented it to his grandfather without a word.

Now Grampa had become used to being one of the first to see Billy's paintings. He had never heard very much about any of them. He chose not to. And Billy never pushed. But for some reason, when his grandfather saw this one, he asked the fateful question. Maybe he was distracted by something he was watching on television and he wasn't thinking, or it was just a rhetorical question, or maybe there's a greater reason for the timing and the content of the question. In any event, he asked it.

"What's this one all about, Billy?"

Without another word, or a preface of any sort, Billy recited the poem from memory.

Freedom

Poison tipped
White lies
Fly Swiftly
Their whispered hissings
Silently decry
My burgundy dark deeds
These arrows drunk
With excessive wine
Still easily find
Their mark
Sharp merciless fangs
Drag me to the ground
Biting wounding louts
Have found me out
Pleading for release
I am left bleeding
Deep blue eons of time
Confine me find me
In a beggar's grip
But then I am delivered
Before the queen of kindness
Who melts my chains
Lays claim to my sanity
And grants my
Freedom

Grampa actually listened. Then he kind of off-handedly asked Billy who the Queen of Kindness was and how he could meet her. He said it with a laugh, but Billy heard his opening.

Grampa had spent the last few months in a daze, since Nana had been gone. And he had spent many years in a dulled consciousness, wracked by guilt and shame, and anger. He had given up on any sort of redemption and had decided long ago, as you know, that he didn't want anything to do with God. He didn't think about God. He didn't believe in any such thing as God. But the Queen of Kindness was somehow a title that intrigued him. He didn't relate that to God in any way. Billy would, though.

He asked his grandfather if it would be all right to invite his father over for dinner that night. Billy said he would like to show him and his mother his new painting. He told his grandfather that he would tell them all about the Queen of Kindness over dinner.

His grandfather started to resist and say that Ron wouldn't come over, anyway. Ron hadn't come near the house when Rachael was around, or even spoken one word to her since she came back from Florida.

And his grandfather told him that he had only asked a curious question and he didn't want any serious answer. He knew that Billy could go on and on about the story behind his paintings. Grampa had heard a lot of the stories, or at least pieces of them. For the most part, he tried to ignore them. But every so often he'd hear a tidbit from the kitchen, when Billy was talking to his mother, and that would resonate a bit within him. He did his best to just shake any resonance off and forget it. But some of it was rubbing off, even on him.

Billy convinced his grandfather that he could talk his father into coming over. So, Billy arranged for dinner. Rachael was a little uneasy at the thought of Ron coming over, but quite a bit of time had gone by since she came home, and they did have a past history and a son they shared. So she said she would be OK with Ron coming over.

Ron adamantly refused to come over when Billy told him what he had planned. But Billy took the upper hand and got very strong with his father. Billy even told Ron to get over his selfishness and do something for his son for a change. That did it. Ron agreed to come over for dinner.

Now, Billy's grandparent's house, where he grew up, had a kitchen in which almost every meal was served, and where they ate every day. There was also a formal dining room where they had holiday dinners, or where they sat down to eat when a larger group of family and friends were invited in for dinner.

Billy spent the afternoon setting up the dining room. He not only put out a formal setting of dishes and silverware, he set up a show of the nine paintings he had completed. He definitely had something up his sleeve beyond an extended family dinner.

Rachael had taken a job in a local dress shop, and she didn't come home until around six, usually. Ron was still doing carpentry and light hauling with his pick-up, so his schedule was pretty flexible. Grampa was home all the time, so he was ready to eat at a five on the button every day, like he had done forever, it seemed. Rachael would just grab a snack at night, most of the time. Billy told them all that dinner would be served at six.

Billy had gotten into cooking since he came back to live with his grandfather. He grew up spending a lot of time in the kitchen to stay out of his grandfather's way, and Nana used to put him to work cutting up veggies, or watching the timer for stuff cooking on the stove, or stirring sauces and gravies. He was pretty comfortable in the kitchen to begin with, so cooking was natural to him.

He also found that as his ability to paint improved, the colors of food, and the smells and textures, came more and more alive and appealing to him. Cooking became another creative outlet for him. He didn't think of it that way at first, but one day it hit him how creative cooking could be. From then on, he had a lot more fun cooking, and it never seemed like a chore to him.

Billy did something else with cooking that his family and friends really enjoyed, even though they found it a little strange. He would show up with a roast or some fresh seafood and ask if he could cook dinner for them.

Can you imagine someone you know showing up to visit and asking if they could cook dinner for you – and even bringing the main dish? It was kind of a joke around his family and friends, but there was also something very loving and intimate about it that they enjoyed very much.

So, Billy was busy at work preparing his gourmet dinner and art show for his family, all afternoon. Ron came in early, around five. He went in and talked with Grampa while Billy scurried around the kitchen, and back and forth to the dining room. Ron asked Grampa to come out to the camp sometime. He hadn't been out there for a long time, and Ron said he would love to spend some time with him. They both had softened toward each other. Ron had been particularly eager to mend fences with Grampa, and Ron ran errands for him and took him for rides and grocery shopping with Billy every so often.

So they chatted away for about an hour before Rachael showed up. When she came in and saw Ron, she visibly winced and dropped her head just a bit. Ron hadn't really taken a good look at her since her return, and he was somewhat shaken to realize how weathered and beaten, and old for her age she looked. A part of him still saw her as beautiful. And when she looked at him the way she did, and dropped her head like that, it touched off a new feeling of compassion within him.

But he steeled himself against any show of emotion. He nodded nonchalantly and looked away. Rachael came over and gave her father a hug. That was a new ritual that Rachael had begun since coming home.

She shared cooking duties with Billy and did a lot of the cleaning around the house. And her heart went out to her father when she saw how devastated he was by the loss of her mother.

She reached out for him one day when she spotted a particularly downtrodden look on his face, and he held onto her for a long, long time. Rachael's heart softened toward her father, and probably toward life in general that day.

Since then, she hugged him every time she prepared to leave the house, and every time she came home. Billy did the same. So there was a lot of hugging going on in that household.

By the time Billy announced that dinner was ready, Rachael and Ron had exchanged a few words and the air in the house was already lightening up. Billy had set the table with serving dishes all in place, and he had set his paintings up, each on their own easel, framing the bay window at the end of the dining room.

It was early evening and the setting sun cast an amber glow over the entire dining room. Billy had set a carafe of red wine and a carafe of white wine side by side, next to a platter of stacked, golden yellow corn on the cob.

The centerpiece platter held four bright red Maine lobsters evenly spaced around a mountain of steamed clams. The lobsters and clams were steaming hot, and a mist rose up from the table that gave the room an otherworldly look.

Billy had sprinkled fresh kale to garnish the lobster and clam combination, and to contrast the bright red lobsters with a touch o reen. Also on the table were two dark brown woven wood baskets, ned with deep purple cloth napkins. The baskets were filled and iled high with lightly browned rolls.

At each place setting Billy had folded robin egg blue napkins 1 a pyramid shape and placed them in the middle of bright white lates. Clear custard cups held hot melted butter at each setting.

The intensely bright yellow warm color of the melted butter nowed through the clear glass cups and reflected off the white plates nd silverware, sending splashes of light off in different directions round the table. The creamy ivory color of the tablecloth seemed to bsorb and soften all of the colors of the food and dishes.

Of course, Ron and Grampa barely noticed the artful presen-ation, but Rachael raved about it as she sat down. About the time she ad reached her chair, she noticed the new painting and asked Billy bout it.

"It's about the Queen of Kindness," Grampa said with a toticeable pride that he was in the know before Rachael.

Billy always showed each of them his paintings as he finished hem, and he offered as much about them as they seemed to be able o comfortably hear.

Sometimes he recited the poem to them and sometimes he lidn't. Usually when he did they would just smile with a kind of blank ook, not wanting to say to Billy that they had no idea about what the painting was supposed to represent or what the poem was trying to ay.

And it wasn't so much that they didn't see anything in the painting or hear anything in the poem, it was just that they didn't want to get Billy started on his story again.

In each of their own personal ways and for reasons of their own, Grampa, Ron and Rachael were afraid, or embarrassed, or at

least uncomfortable with talking about Billy's episode when he w.
ten, and especially with all his talk about God.

Billy knew this well, and almost always let them off the hoc
by talking about the colors and the shapes of the paintings as the focu
of attention, and leaving it at that. But tonight would be different, an
everybody knew it. It was in the air.

Rachael was hoping that Billy wasn't doing this to try to ge
her and Ron back together. She and Ron had not even spoken to eac
other for months. Ron avoided her at the funeral, and pretended no
to notice her on the several occasions that their paths had crossed i
town or at the grocery store over the past few months. Rachael wa
relatively content to stay at home, read and cook, and sew.

She was enjoying her work at the dress shop and would pic
up fashion magazines and fabric whenever she could. She was desigr
ing dresses, creating them at home, and even selling an occasion:
dress at the shop.

She wasn't passionate about it, the way Billy was about h
painting, but she was really very good at it and received a lot c
encouragement from the woman who owned the shop.

Ron was thinking pretty much the same thing, hoping tha
Billy wasn't trying to patch things up. Ron had held on to a self-righ
eous anger about Rachael's up and leaving him, ten days before the
wedding. It had been more than a dozen years since that happenec
and he would still drift into thinking about it every so often, an
would find himself mad as a hornet, reliving it.

There was no way he was going to set himself up for ye
another fall. And besides, he had a nice relationship with a youn
woman who worked at the lumberyard where he picked up stuff fc
his never-ending projects at camp.

He had only come to dinner at Billy's insistence. But he wa

glad to see that he could actually face Rachael without all the old anger coming up. It helped him to see her face to face, instead of just listening to those old lions in his mind. Seeing her helped him to let go of some of the negative images he held in his mind. He was really surprised that they were actually able to exchange a couple of pleasantries before dinner.

Grampa was expecting an art show, and he, too, suspected that part of Billy's plan this evening, was to try and reconcile Ron and Rachael. He was used to Billy coming to him with a drawing or a painting he had just done.

Since he had been a little kid, Billy was always running up to show everybody a new cartoon or something else he had drawn. So, the presentation of the paintings around the room was not entirely new to Grampa, or Ron, or Rachael. And neither was the dinner presentation. They knew this was a part of Billy's world as well.

So, as Rachael looked around the table and complimented Billy on the beautiful arrangement and presentation, Ron and Grampa added a couple of mumbles that acknowledged Billy's efforts as well.

They joined hands around the table, as was the custom that Billy had instituted from the time he came back to live with Grampa. And Billy said grace, as was his custom. He said it with the lighthearted sense of humor that they had also become accustomed to hearing from him.

"Well, Lord, I know I'm surrounded by a bunch of unbelievers who think that the youngest member of their family is totally nuts. But I know that you have a sense of humor and I know that you are infinitely patient.

"So please warm our hearts, that we might find forgiveness in them. Quiet our minds, that we might feel inner peace, and zap our taste buds, that we might enjoy this food, which you know wa cooked with love, by the way. Let us cherish this time together as family. Amen"

Ron wasn't as used to hearing Billy speak this way as Racha and Grampa were, and he looked over at Billy with a strange litt smile. When Ron caught Billy's eye, Billy smiled back. At th moment, Ron felt a wave of pride for his son, and comfort in his pre ence that somehow felt different this evening.

Things were beginning to feel different for everyone at th table. Billy had slipped a little phrase into his prayer that was pu posely intended to plant a seed, and set the stage for what was t come.

Rachael reached for the red wine and as she tipped the bottl slightly, the setting sun caught it just right and reflected a beam c light into Ron's eye. He blinked and turned his head. When he di that, he caught the light also shining on one of Billy's paintings. Whe Ron looked back at the table, he did a double take back to the paint ing.

Ron stood up and walked over to the display of paintings without a word. Grampa turned to see what he was doing. Racha poured her glass of wine and looked up to see Ron looking at Billy painting and then back at the table setting. Billy was kind of please at his father's keen interest, all of a sudden. But he didn't think to much of it until his father spoke.

"Look at these paintings that Billy did, and then look at th table the way the sun hits all the colors. They're the same. The colo are all the same. They're..."

You could tell Ron wanted to say more, but couldn't find th words. He stopped and sat back down at the table with kind of a embarrassed smile. Grampa and Billy and Rachael were a littl stunned at Ron's new artistic sensibilities. This wasn't like him at all. Things went quiet while they started to dig into dinner. Then it hit Billy.

That morning at the castle, the first morning Billy came down to breakfast, he had the same reaction as Ron just had. He saw that the colors of the food on the table, and the reflected light from the sun, were the same as the colors in the paintings in his room.

Connections came rushing into Billy's mind like a huge tapestry of many colors being woven at super high speed. He was thinking so many thoughts and experiencing so many insights at the same time.

There are patterns everywhere. It is our awareness of them that makes all the difference. There are magic moments always happening. And something as simple as a light reflecting colors can touch new sensibilities with us, and awaken us to a new reality of beauty in this world.

There's a harmony and a connection in all of nature and in all of life. We are all connected, bound together and tightly woven into the fabric that makes up our life.

It all flashed by so fast. It all made so much clear sense to Billy. He felt like he might splinter into light at that very moment. The sense of awe, joy and contentment he knew at that moment were beyond description.

Billy had planned all along to use this evening as a platform for his art show, and as an opportunity to talk about the Queen of Kindness to his family. His intent all along was to help them bridge the gap between them as a family. And, he knew that he would work in his special story of how the gap between them could be closed by the God of love and kindness that he knew, and wanted them to know. He wanted everyone to know.

That was clearly his mission in life, and it's current ran

through every word, and act, and thought in Billy's life. His family had come to know that in a way, and accepted it in a way. But they hadn't come to understand it in a way that Billy wanted to share it.

He wanted them to share the experiential knowledge of God that he had been so privileged to receive. He was frustrated at times that he couldn't just hand them his experience of coming into God's presence like you would hand someone a gold nugget.

But suddenly, from that visual insight that Ron experienced, Billy realized that he couldn't push, or rush, or coax, or convince any-one into awareness. They had to come to it on their own. They would see when they were ready to see. People are where they are in their development in life. Billy could set the stage, the way he set up his art show, the way he painted the paintings, the way he told his stories, the way he set the table. But the director of the play was "upstairs". And God would assign the parts at his choosing.

Suddenly Billy was relieved of his duty to save the world. He couldn't quite understand how he got this from the way Ron reacted. But Billy got it.

He could plant the seeds, but God would cause them to open, take root, and burst forth into the light. Now Billy could continue with his plans for the evening, with a deeper understanding of his pur-pose.

Billy thought to himself that he loved the way God works. Billy had a plan that he was pretty proud of, but God had a bigger plan, way beyond what Billy had thought or imagined.

"For dessert," Billy started to say, as everyone held onto their stomachs and waved off dessert, "we have, the glorious art work and narrative by a soon to be discovered, rising young artist – me."

They laughed as Billy walked over to his display of paintings. Billy was on stage, once again, and back to his story:

You remember this painting. It's called *Transformation.* It was the first one I did in this style. I don't expect you to remember the words that went with it. But it is about what happened to me after I first fell through the ice.

That transformation, that incredibly joyful experience of pure peace of mind is available to anyone who longs for it. Now hold on to your seats, I won't go back over that, just yet.

And then *Silence.* I kept silent for a long time. I had a lot to learn, and Mom protected me. Thanks, Mom. But when the paintings came back to me, and spoke to me, I knew that I couldn't and wouldn't be silent anymore.

Devotion is the title of my next painting. This one I'm still learning about. But my devotion to what I am going to do with my life is clear.

This next painting is called *Elation.* This took me a long time to learn about. When puberty set in, and the hormones raged, nothing was important as sex. I don't mean to embarrass you, or upset you. It's just a fact of life.

This is an aspect of life that we enjoy more deliriously, and suffer guilt about more seriously than any other. Enough said. But I came into an awareness, had an experience that, for me, is the ultimate man human experience in life. It is better and more fulfilling than sex. OK, I'll move on before you get total indigestion.

Passion came to me as I spoke to you at Nana's funeral. This is about a passion for life, a passion for experiencing life at all levels. All levels. It's about coming to know more than we thought we knew, and hanging onto it with every fiber of our being.

The next painting, *Forgiveness,* comes in a good place. The elation we feel, the passion we feel, can bring us to unbelievable heights

of emotion, cause us great joy, and at the same time, leads us int
doing things that afterward leave us feeling deep regret and a burnin
need for forgiveness. Forgiving ourselves is the toughest part. I kno
you know that to be true.

Anticipation is about a journey back home, back to a place w
all knew once before. We may have forgotten it for a time, but whe
we intuit that we are on our way back home, the thrill of anticipatio
pushes us eagerly home. We each have our own journey here. And w
each have our own means, or vehicle, by which we return.

And then there's *The Breeze*, a wonderfully refreshing flow c
air. But it also represents those hateful words and judgment an
unforgiveness that we feel from other people.

It's also about the concerns we have with what other peopl
will think. That can bring us to our knees and make us feel totall
unworthy. But there is a victory over this, a way to get out from und
the emotional grip of what other people think. We can be free of a
of that, and ride the breeze in a time of refreshing joy.

So, now we come to the new painting of the day, *Freedom*
And now we come to my reason for calling this little family gatherin
I want you to meet the Queen of Kindness. She grants freedom. An
that is the reason for the name of this painting.

When I told Grampa the words that go with this painting an
about the Queen of Kindness who grants freedom, he asked me abou
this Queen of Kindness. He even jokingly said he would like to mee
her. I would like you all to meet her. I assure you, she wants to mee
you.

I'm your son and your grandson, and of course, I don't kno
all the details of your lives. But I do know what we've talked about fo
years. I know how mad and hurt you were when Mom left, Dad.
know that Mom feels like God doesn't love her. And I know tha

Grampa is uncomfortable with any mention of God. I'm not sure why.

Dad, when I lived with you, you let me do things that you would never have allowed if you were not so caught up in your anger and hurt. And you certainly did things that you would never do if you were not so upset and discouraged about what had happened.

Mom, you and I have talked a lot about how your life has gone and your reason for doing things that you have done. You've told me over and over how sorry you are for what happened, and how guilty you feel for causing others so much pain.

And Grampa, I still remember that day that you left me at camp and drove off because I said you were mean. I heard you sputter about that to Nana months after it happened.

Well, you know what, everyone in life has regrets. Everyone would change some things they've done or not done in life. Most people feel lost and quietly desperate at times. Everyone who stops and thinks about it, thinks of a time when they did something unkind and thoughtless. It's part of the human condition and the experience of being alive.

But with all of this, life is an awesome and wonderful experience, and when you are granted freedom, you will find a fullness of joy that nothing on earth can take away. You will still experience storms and difficulties, but in your heart, beneath all of the circumstances of life, will be this light of love and joy that can never be disturbed.

The secret to re-discovering joy and fulfillment in this life is to meet the Queen of Kindness. She can melt the chains of regret and unforgiveness. She can grant you entrance into her kingdom of peace and joy and beauty. And she can do that right here, right now. If you haven't figured it out, the Queen of Kindness is an aspect of God.

Now at this point Grampa was squirming, but Billy wasn't about to stop now. What he did at this point was pretty outrageous. He reminded them that he had spent all day preparing the meal, and now he wanted something in return. The something he wanted was humility.

Billy asked Grampa to look at Ron and Rachael and ask them to please forgive him for everything and anything he had ever done to upset them or hurt them. In the midst of this, Grampa reminded them that he had given them the camp. But Billy cleared his throat and Grampa went back to asking them for their forgiveness.

Then Ron and Rachael did the same, each to the other two people at the table. And as for Ron and Rachael, Billy listened quietly as they asked him for forgiveness.

Billy looked at Grampa, and without a word from Billy, Grampa quietly asked Billy to forgive him for anything he had ever done to hurt him in any way.

Finally, Billy spoke to each of them in the same way and asked them to please forgive him. After Billy finished, an absolute quiet fell over the room. Simple nods of acknowledgement granted the kindness of forgiveness to everyone.

The sun had gone down by now and the light in the room was dim. The lights had not been turned on, but a definite glow filled the room.

Bliss

You think
You can escape this life
Without a mistake
Without a forfeiture of
Sky blue pink
That will cost you
An arm and leg
Not for damned sure
Eternity in the dregs
Of a fiery hell
Well of all people
You should know better
Blood sweating wretch
Your prison of regret
Will never let you go
What do I perceive
In those misty eyes
Who is it this time
Who arrives at my domain
Those keys won't fit
You're artistry is in vain
There is no power in a kiss
But what is this
Bliss

b l i s s

Chapter Fifteen – Bliss

"Thank you, Billy," Rachael said very softly, as she and Billy began to clear the table. Ron and Grampa had not spoken another word. They just got up after sitting at the table for ten minutes and walked into the living room. Grampa turned on the television and he and Ron sat silently staring at whatever was on the screen.

On one of his trips back into the dining room for dishes, Billy thought for a moment that he saw a shadow of his old friend William and the sweet young woman named Karen, whom he recognized from the castle, standing by the paintings.

The image lasted just long enough to remind him of Karen and how peaceful and gentle a person she seemed to always be. She was the one who had talked to Billy about the painting named Freedom.

Karen was tiny, with small facial features, and green eyes that could only be described as the kindest eyes he had ever seen. Kind eyes, he remembered, just the eyes you would expect from someone who knew all about the Queen of Kindness.

Karen wore a burgundy cape, with red piping and red tassels at the end of the piping that tied around her shoulders. The flowing cape gave the impression that she floated as she walked.

Her movements were slow and graceful and delicate. H[ ]voice was as soft as the kitten she seemed to be always carrying. Sh[ ]would stroke the kitten and nuzzle her nose down into the kitten's fu[ ]every few minutes. That's how Billy remembered her.

Her exact words did not come back to Billy, but he knew tha[ ]she was the one who had talked to him about the releasing power [ ]giving and receiving forgiveness.

She had made it a point to say many times, that the Queen [ ]Kindness reigns forever, and she always melts the chains of everyon[ ]who is brought before her, no matter what they have been accused [ ]doing.

"No matter what," she would say sometimes, when she woul[ ]see Billy staring out of his window.   No other words than that, lik[ ]she knew that he was thinking of some regret or failure on his par[ ]He had heard that voice quite a few times over the last ten or twelv[ ]years. And they were always deliciously sweet and comforting.

Now you might think that Billy's performance over dinne[ ]and his show would change everything immediately and there woul[ ]be peace and love and forgiveness in the family, and they would liv[ ]happily ever after.

Well, it didn't work that way. It seems that this kind of posi[ ]tive action that Billy undertook sometimes provokes an opposite neg[ ]ative reaction to offset it. That's not true. Love is stronger than hate o[ ]fear. Forgiveness is stronger than regret. The positive action wins ou[ ]in the end.

But there is a battle, and Billy knew that the lions never giv[ ]up totally. And certainly, people will talk and judge and condemn.

Rachael and Ron did patch things up, and even re-kindle[ ]their youthful friendship to a degree that neither ever expected to se[ ]in their lives again. They truly did forgive each other. So Billy's sho[ ] did wonders for them, and they never forgot it.

As for the battle, well, Grampa started having horrible nightmares, beginning the night of Billy's dinner and show. Of course, the heavy and rich food could have had a lot to do with it, but the nightmares were hellish. Grampa even called for Billy in the night to come and sit with him for a while.

Grampa thought he was going to die, and that he was being shown previews of the hell that awaited him for eternity. This was a lot worse than thinking of death as just lights out for eternity.

Billy felt responsible for this turn of events. He thought that his words had stirred some old fears and doubts up. And he was right. Like so many people who begin to reach out once again, and brave a journey along a spiritual path in search of God, or peace of mind or some ineffable change of heart, something dreadful and sad happens.

The lions dredge up old false and inaccurate images from the stories passed down to people from parrots who don't know what they're talking about.

If Billy hadn't been so determined not to let the lions of his own mind, or anyone else on earth ever deter him again from telling and teaching and painting about what he knew to be true, he might have kept quiet. Instead, in the face of what was happening, he spoke even more boldly to his grandfather.

Billy boldly suggested to Grampa that he had dredged up old images and thoughts of heaven and hell from his childhood days of Sunday school. He had been taught the standard old line of a God who watches over us, but he had also heard of a God who is ready to send us to hell for doing something wrong. Like the rest of us, Grampa had done enough things that he regretted, that he decided long ago that he didn't want anything to do with this God.

Christian scripture clearly tells of a hell that exists, all right, but it says that it exists for the enemy of God, Satan, and his followers, to use their words.

In these Christians stories and in many other cultural and religious stories, the dark place, or hell, is for those who oppose the truth of God's sovereign power. And sovereign power simply means a power that is on it's own, that nothing can touch or be greater than. That part, of a power greater than we are as individuals is a tough one for the ego.

It is a power for good, the power of love. A God of love does not send his creation, any of his creation, to a fiery hell. That's not a Christian God or any kind of God. That is a lie from the lions of fear and doubt. God is love.

Billy talked evening after evening, sometimes late into the night, and sometimes when Grampa got him up in the middle of the night. On one of these occasions, Billy used the word, bliss, to describe the state of mind that knowing God brings. As soon as the word came out of his mouth, he stopped talking and started painting. He literally bounded up three stairs at a time to his room.

In a couple of hours, he brought the painting and the poem to his grandfather.

Bliss

You think
You can escape
Without a mistake
A forfeiture of
Sky blue pink
That will cost you
An arm and leg

For damned sure
Eternity in the dregs
Of a fiery hell
Well of all people
You should know better
Blood sweating wretch
Your prison of regret
Will never let you go
What do I perceive
In those misty eyes
Who is it this time
Who arrives at my domain
Those keys won't fit
You're artistry is in vain
There is no power in a kiss
But what is this
Bliss

"You see, Grampa, do you see?" Billy said breathlessly. "Even hell cannot prevail against God's love. Jesus said that he holds the keys to heaven and hell, and that even the gates of hell cannot prevail against him.

"Jonathan told me that. He was a man at the castle who knew a lot about Jesus, and what he really taught.

"I know you don't like me to talk about my time at the castle, Grampa, but you know me, you know how I feel. You must have heard me talking to Mom and Nana. And you listened to me at the dinner that time with Mom and Dad. Grampa, God is real. You can know that, too. I can show you."

Those last few words that came out of Billy's mouth stunned

him more than they did his grandfather. Billy had never said that to anyone. He talked and talked about his experience and his sure knowledge of the reality of God. And he had very clear visions of the paintings and the stories and poems. But he had never said that he could show God to anyone. That thought never occurred to him. But he had said it. How could that have come out of his mouth, he thought.

As he went within with this question, his mind went quiet. There was none of the internal chatter, no lions, no words of any sort. Billy closed his eyes.

And once again, he was in that most blissful of interior places, in God's deliciously comforting presence. Love washed over him, bringing peace of mind, utter tranquility and more, an absolutely beyond-words joy of knowing that God was with him at that moment.

This was not some abstract thought, some fuzzy notion or wish. God was with Billy. God's presence enveloped and held Billy. God and Billy, knowing each other, fully and completely, that was Billy's experience. Words cannot come close.

The next thing Billy knew or felt was a warm kiss on his forehead. And then that time, that very special time with William and Sharon, came back.

Sharon was holding a rose. She and William were talking to Billy about the painting and poem called, "Bliss". This particular piece had a fierceness about it. The words were powerful and forceful. They seemed to blast fury and fire. They were words like people had heard from the lions. And he was right. Sharon confirmed his thought as she spoke.

'Billy, as people who are seeking God's touch move closer to that experience, the lions step up their ferocity. The lions of fear and doubt roar the loudest and speak the harshest words, the closer one comes. They know that if they can discourage someone at the last moment, they will almost never come back.

"These people who are turned away at the last moment are the ones with the strongest ego and pride. They hate to admit to the possibility that there is someone or something greater than they are as individuals.

"They give in to the fear, and then they become powerful and forceful in their own right. But there's no kindness and compassion, there's anger and disappointment, and pride of self.

"They become so bitter that they stand against anyone who declares their freedom. They try to beat them down, and discourage them just like they are discouraged.

"They do not know the truth, and they do not believe in any other truth than the limited despair that rules their lives. It is very hard to turn these people around. They are unknowing allies of the lions."

Now remember, William was the one usually teaching about the lions, and the people in the castle were the ones teaching about the paintings. This time, Sharon was the one talking about the lions, and William was just listening to her and nodding his head in agreement. But what Sharon did next brought it all into balance.

The three of them, William, Sharon and Billy, were now standing at the entrance to the castle. The lions were silent, as they usually were when William was present. Sharon leaned over and kissed one lion and then the next on the top of their heads. Actually she kissed them on their foreheads, right in the middle. Then she turned and handed the rose she was holding to Billy.

Billy had forgotten all about this event, and it hadn't crossed his mind once since that time so many years ago. But it came back vividly.

He remembered how he giggled to see Sharon kiss the lions. He blinked, and for a brief moment he saw the image of Karen holding her kitten. Then he saw the proudly erect lions bow their heads and settle down on their front legs and paws.

"All it takes is a kiss, Billy," Sharon said as she watched Billy's amazement. "A holy kiss is all it takes. Not just any kiss, it must be a holy kiss. A holy kiss is something very, very special to give.

"The kiss must be as delicate as a flower, and you must be very, very still inside. The holy kiss is a messenger of God's love. The kiss must only be given to someone who is ready to receive it. You will know. You will see a need and a very real reason for bestowing the holy kiss.

"The kiss may be an actual physical kiss, or you may send it with your heart. Your mind must be totally in God's presence. You will know when that presence is absolutely pure and clear. And you will know when it is not. So, don't thoughtlessly send any of these special kisses.

"Only those who are ready for a touch of God's love experientially, in their hearts, will receive it. Each one will bring bliss to the person who receives it. And some of them will come to realize that they, too, can bestow this special kiss, this holy kiss." That was all Sharon said. Then William spoke.

"You will not remember any of this time with Sharon, and the secret of the holy kiss, until you are fully ready and fully devoted to your purpose in life. When you are, this time with Sharon will come back to you clearly. Use it wisely."

The sound of Grampa's voice brought Billy back from this time.

"Billy, don't talk like that. No one can show anyone God. No one can see God, " Grampa's voice came through. "Get me my slippers will you? I'm going back to bed."

Billy was going to tell his grandfather that he wasn't talking about physical senses, about seeing God with your eyes, he was talking about inner vision, and an experience of the heart. But he just smiled and did what he had done hundreds of times before.

He got Grampa his slippers. Grampa noticed the kind and peaceful look on Billy's face as he put each slipper on. Billy stopped to rub each foot, the way Grampa liked, before putting on his slippers.

They both went back to bed, but Billy didn't go right to sleep. He kept thinking about the awesome reality of what he now remembered. He could open the door. He could bestow a holy kiss. Did that really mean that he could be the catalyst to bring the incredible bliss he knew to someone else?

It didn't seem real. It didn't seem possible. But the idea warmed him to his very core, and the ecstatic feelings were there, the belief that it just might be true was beginning to be there. He couldn't think of anything else. Eventually he drifted off to sleep. And his dreams were sweet beyond belief.

Sunrise At Two Lions

Ecstasy

Mysteries of the moon
Hide the truth
Of visionary sight
Deep dark aching
Black and blue misery
Stirs embers of regret
White hot hopeless breath
Inspires yet another step
Flashes of burnt anger
Saturate the sky
Illuminate the fear
Threaten to inflict
A mortal wound
Stronger fiercer
Don't come near
Don't come near
But it's much too late
The cantaloupe antelope
Gives me a ride
And I arrive
At the peak
Unblemished
Unbridled
Ecstatic

e c s t a s y

Chapter Sixteen – Ecstasy

Ron was shaking Billy's shoulder trying to wake him up. Ron couldn't believe how soundly Billy was sleeping. He stopped to check his breathing for a second, not really seriously worried, but concerned enough to check. He had been shaking Billy for a couple of minutes and saying his name over and over without a response.

Billy was breathing. He was just sleeping so peacefully that he had gone into a very deep sleep. He opened his eyes to see his father's concerned expression. Billy smiled to see his father standing there, so close to him. And then he remembered that they were going to look at new trucks that day. It was Saturday.

As Billy got up, got dressed and came downstairs, he felt strangely very much like he felt that first morning back at the castle. That feeling was intensified as he came into the kitchen and saw the breakfast his mother had prepared.

Two pitchers of orange juice and fresh-baked cinnamon rolls with white frosting setting on a big raspberry platter reminded him of his first breakfast at the castle. He loved the colors, as always.

He smiled a look of approval at his mother and went over an gave her a hug. Ron raised his eyebrows with a quick motion, twice He did once for the impressive cooking that surprised him, and a sec ond time to see the warm affection between Billy and Rachael.

She asked Ron and Billy to sit down and have something t eat before heading out to look at trucks. She told them that Gramp had already had his coffee and a roll, and had gone out for a walk.

"A walk, you're kidding?" Billy said, as more of a question c surprise than a statement.

Grampa never went out for walks. Billy could never remem ber a time that Grampa went out for a walk, and he couldn't believ it. Grampa went to work, back when he used to work, came home an watched television, went to sleep and that was his day.

Now he hardly ever got out of his chair in the living room Only rarely did he change his routine. An occasional fishing trip or rare visit to family and friends, or a trip to shop for groceries, wa about the only change in Grampa's daily regimen that Billy had eve seen.

Before Billy and Ron had finished breakfast, Grampa cam back from his walk. As he came in, he took a deep loud inhale and sai what a gorgeous day it was out there, and did anybody notice th incredible blue in the sky today.

This was not Grampa. It couldn't be. Grampa had mope around the house for months, hardly ever speaking to anyone else, o ever starting a conversation. He tolerated, and secretly enjoyed, th exchange of hugs from Billy and Rachael but other than that h watched television. And that was about it, since Nana's passing.

But it was him, bright-eyed and bushy-tailed like no one i the house at the time ever remembered seeing in their lifetime. The poked at each other and tried not to let Grampa see how surprised they were. Ron did another quick eyebrow move. And Billy gave him a quick wink.

"What did you do to him?" Ron asked as he and Billy pulled out of the driveway. Billy just shrugged his shoulders, but Ron wasn't ready to dismiss it that easily. "Do you think that he's finally gotten over Nana's accident?"

"No, he'll never get over that. But it's nice to see him come alive again. I still can't get over him going for a walk, and them coming in the way he did. That was just incredible."

"You're right about that. But, I do know that you've been working on him. He actually listened while you talked about the Queen of Kindness painting, even when you said that Queen of Kindness is an aspect of God."

Now here was another shocker. Ron never acknowledged Billy's talk about God, and Billy never pushed it on him in the slightest way. But here was Ron, opening it up.

He went on to uncharacteristically tell Billy that he knew he was a very special son. He told Billy that he was very proud of him, and he hoped Billy knew that he had always loved him a lot.

Billy joked about somebody putting something in the water today, and asked what the heck was going on with everyone today.

Ron obviously wanted to talk. He talked about how devastated he was when Billy was missing and they were afraid they would never see him again, and how incredibly ecstatic he was when Billy came back home safe and sound.

Ron had to break the serious and touching tone for a bit, in order to stay composed and not get too emotional. So he told Billy that he wasn't so sure of the "sound" part. As he said that he reached over and messed up Billy's hair. If you've been paying attention, you might guess what happened in that instant.

"So, Billy, you have only two more paintings to pick," Willia announced, as he gave Billy a quick rub on the top of the head "You've been here for some time now, and it is getting close to the tin when you will return home.

"Much of what you will have to take back with you becam known to you in that instant you came into the light. The beginnin of wisdom blossomed and absolute clarity was realized by you the da you came into God's presence, in that moment you came into th holiest of places available to us in the living time.

"That clarity and knowledge of God's reality, and the natur of God's character will always be known to you now. But as you g back to your time with your family, you will need to grow in wisdon and learn life lessons.

"You will need to mature and learn, as you have, how to de with the lions of fear and doubt, and especially the people who hav been robbed by fear and doubt, whom you will encounter.

"The most powerful and lasting lessons, and therefore th most difficult, will come through your own difficulty with fear an doubt. Your own mistakes will ultimately be your most powerfu teachers. The bigger mistake will be to temporarily forget the lesson you have learned here.

"Your own concepts, and the concepts of others that you wi acquire and adopt as your own, will present themselves as solid truth But this need to arrive at solid truth with the thinking mind can be snare and a trap that will cause you despair.

"People who insist that they have arrived at an objective truth can risk shutting themselves off from a deeper truth. And those wh shut themselves off, shut themselves off from kindness and caring, an et rules and expectations rule their lives.

"They protect their exclusive truth the way they protect their material possessions. They come to care more for material things more than they do for other people. This is where much of the world's misery begins.

"You will be more sensitive to people's needs than before you came here, Billy. But you are only ten years old. As you mature, much more sensitivity and creativity will come to you.

"And when you come to clearly realize your purpose for coming here, and more importantly, your reason for returning home, you will know what this time has been about. No one will be able to hide this vision from you.

"You will meet people who will deny the reality of what you know, but they do not know experientially what you know. So you will be able to encounter them, and no matter how threatening they are, you will be able to hold onto your vision and your experience.

"There will come a time, when a passion and a fire will overtake you. It will fill you with a resolve and a purpose so undeniable that no power on earth will be able to discourage you or contain you. That will come later."

With that final word, William stood up and walked Billy back to the castle. They passed the now silent lions. Billy went right upstairs and immediately took one of the last two paintings off the wall in his room. Somehow this one always frightened him a bit.

The colors were deep and intense. Billy always intuitively felt that this painting represented a fierce battle. He was right about the battle . William would tell him about the final outcome.

Billy took the painting downstairs. And when he reached the bottom of the stairs he saw a man wearing a soft flowing robe that reached the floor. The robe was an unusual, soft orange color, more

like the color of the inside of a cantaloupe. Billy thought that this wa
someone he had not met, but when he took a second look, it surprise
him to see that it was William.

He had never seen William with his long dark hair pulled t
the back of his head. This style changed his looks quite a bit. And
took Billy a second take to recognize him.

He had also never seen William in a robe like this. Bil
thought it was beautiful color, and he smiled brightly to see Willia
looking like this. Billy asked him if he knew who would tell him abou
this second to last painting.

Well, this was finally the painting that William would tal
about. Knowing that Billy would pick this one was why William ha
changed his appearance and put on the cantaloupe-colored robe. H
recited the poem on the back of the painting as Billy turned it over t
read it.

Ecstasy

Mysteries of the moon
Hide the truth
Of visionary sight
Deep dark aching
Black and blue misery
Stirs embers of regret
White hot hopeless breath
Inspires yet another step
Flashes of burnt anger
Saturate the sky
Illuminate the fear
Threaten to inflict

A mortal wound
Stronger fiercer
Don't come near
Don't come near
But it's much too late
The cantaloupe antelope
Gives me a ride
And I arrive
At the peak
Unblemished
Unbridled
Ecstatic

"I've told you about this painting in many ways and many times, Billy," William started. "The part I want to tell you about now is the part about being beyond danger, beyond any fear and doubt.

"You are beyond any lasting fear now. The big questions that many people wrestle with all of their lives have faded away and hold no significance for you. You will never fear death. No mortal wound can ever truly threaten you. You have seen through the veil. It is much too late for anyone or anything in life to ever truly threaten you.

"And I will always be there, Billy. Now and forever, I will be by your side. You won't see me, but you will know in your heart that I am there. You may forget for a time, but in times of trouble, you will turn to me. And I will always be there.

"You will face life's difficulties and even life's tragedies. You will most certainly encounter people who will try to stop you from telling about your knowledge and your experience.

"Some will ridicule you. Others will even threaten to cause you physical harm. They will threaten to expose you as a fraud, or expose some terrible sin that you have committed. But do not be intimidated.

"You know who you are, and you know what you have experienced and learned. Nothing they do, and nothing that you will do, can ever change that. You will remember that.

"Those who will judge you for your errors and misdeeds in life, and those who threaten you, are only trying to conceal their own doubts and fears and misdeeds. They feel that they are without God, or unworthy of knowing God.

"They are the ones who need God the most, and they are the ones who need to hear what you have to say. So persist, stay the course. Don't become judgmental like them, and at the same time, don't withhold love from them.

"Understand that they are on a different journey, but everyone is worthy of God's love and eligible for God's forgiveness. They are where they are on their journey.

"You are called to provide light, even for them. Their fear may cause them to try to resist your light, and they will even try to draw you into their darkness. They will try to convince you that even though you once experienced the presence of God, you are no longer worthy to walk in the light, for some reason.

"You will even hear this voice of doubt and accusation, the voice of the lions, inside your own head. Remember, it is hardest to forgive ourselves. Even you will be in danger of deciding that you have lost your light. But that feeling will never last long. And there will come a time when you will not entertain that thought for even a split second. You will know when that comes to you.

"As soon as you look for me, and as many times as you feel lost and look for me, I will be there. And I will give you a ride back to the peak experience that you know. And we will arrive there together unbridled by what others think, unblemished by any fear and doubt, ecstatic."

"Hey, you going to come take a look at this beauty?" Ron's voice sounded distance until Billy realized where he was. They had arrived at the Ford dealership, and Ron knew that they had a brand new black Ford truck on the lot that he wanted to test drive.

It wasn't long before they were back at Grampa's, urging him to come out and take a look. Grampa gladly came out and gave the truck the obligatory slow walk-around. He stroked the fenders, kneeled down for a closer look at the tires, and eventually climbed in the cab.

"This is some vehicle, Billy," Grampa assessed. "Think you can handle it?" Grampa knew that it was a truck that Billy could handle, but he liked to get a reaction from Billy.

He didn't realize that his question struck another chord in Billy's mind. Billy was thinking of the awesome privilege and responsibility that he had been given, and the question of whether or not he could handle it wasn't far from the surface of his mind.

"Hope so. I think I can," Billy fired back.

"Oh, it's beautiful!" came Rachael's voice as she walked up to the window on the driver's side and peered in to take a look at the new truck.

Now even that statement resonated in Billy's heart. He was beginning to hear everything in the context of his new awareness. He noticed while listening to the radio in the truck, as he and Ron were coming to show Grampa, that every song spoke of God's love and the beauty of life.

It was like a game for him, as he waited for the next song. And for five songs in a row, the message was absolutely, clearly the same to him. Everything is beautiful in its own way. God's love is everywhere in its own way. The love we feel for one another is God's love coming through us. That's what the love songs, and all the songs today, were saying to him.

So with everyone so enthusiastic about the new truck, Ron and Billy went back and closed the deal. There were able to drive off in their new truck that very day. They headed out to camp. And on the way, Ron picked up where he had left off earlier in the day.

"That night at the dinner, when you did that art show of your paintings, and then had us all ask for and give each other forgiveness - that changed my life, Billy.

"I know I'm your father, and I'm supposed to teach you about life. But sometimes I think we get it wrong. You have taught me more about life, at your young age, than anyone else I know of, at any age. And I'm in my forties.

"I didn't think I could ever forgive your mother. I didn't even feel like I meant it, when I told her that I forgave her. And I didn't really feel forgiven when you and Mom and Grampa said you forgave me.

"But a couple of days later, I felt it settle in. I really did forgive your mother. And I think she really did forgive me for all the terrible things I said to her. Boy, talk about the kettle calling the pot black. Man! I was awful to her.

"I'm sure you remember some of the things that went on out at camp. I'm really ashamed to even bring them up again. I'm sorry wasn't a better father to you. I tried to be your friend, more than father. I shouldn't have let you do some of those things, let alone encourage them. I cringe every time I think about some of what went on there.

"It wasn't like I didn't know it was wrong, with the drugs and booze, and women, with you only thirteen or fourteen years old. I was just so discouraged and mad at your Mom, and…

"There I go, making excuses. No excuses. I did an awful job, and I feel real bad about it, Billy."

Well, Billy just let Ron go on and on and get it all out. Then he reminded him that he had already forgiven him, and Ron had said he felt forgiven. They went back over a few things, and after a while, Ron and Billy were even able to laugh about a couple of really weird things that went on.

Ron winced a little bit at the mention of one particularly rowdy evening, but Billy reached over and punched his father on the shoulder to lighten him up.

"Dad, I love you a lot," Billy said very directly. He was looking right at his father when he said it. And when Ron turned to acknowledge what Billy had just said, they made eye contact. Ron saw a look in Billy eyes that just melted him. Those words went right to Ron's heart.

They spent the rest of the day lounging around the camp, watching TV, laughing and joking. In the late afternoon Billy offered to go for pizza.

Over pizza, Ron told Billy that while he was gone to pick up the pizza, something unusual had happened. Ron said that while he was waiting, looking out over the lake, he had a sense that he could see the scene of Billy falling through the ice back when he was ten.

Ron kind of shivered as he talked about it, it was that real to him. Then he went on to tell Billy that it felt more like Ron, himself, was re-living what had happened to Billy.

"It was like I was watching you, but then it was me who was falling through the ice. It was really strange. I could feel myself drop and sink down in the cold water. And that's all I remember. I snapped out of it. Weird," Ron said.

They finished their pizza in the peaceful and quiet earl evening at the lake. They had kind of talked themselves out during th day. So they relaxed and watched the golden tones of sunset as the col ors sparkled off the water and through the trees.

As the pink and golden peach tones saturated the sky and col ors streaked through the clouds, Billy heard Ron softly say "Unbelievably beautiful."

When Billy got ready to go home, he asked Ron to drive hin back into town. But Ron was so relaxed and sleepy that he let Bill take the new truck. Ron asked Billy to come back out and pick hin up in the morning and said they'd go out to breakfast. They ende their day together with a warm hug. No words were required. The each knew that they had come much closer together as father and so that day.

Billy stopped at the flower shop on his way home. He picke up a dozen red roses and a new vase to put them in. When he pulle into the driveway in his father's new truck, and stepped out with th flowers in hand, his mother came out to greet him.

"What, do you have a date?" Rachael asked.

"Nope, these are for you," Billy said, as he handed them ove

Rachael came up behind Billy and gave him a quick kiss o the cheek as he was putting the roses in the new vase. He turne around and lifted her right off her feet with a big hug.

Well, over the next few weeks the world of Billy King-Frase and his family went through a lot of change.

His father decided to go back to school to study architecture He had a lot of work in front of him. He had only completed abou two years of college, taking a course here and a course there since hig school. But, for some reason, he had found a new self-confidence an mbition. And he wanted to become an architect.

Billy's grandfather decided to go back to work. He took a real state exam and signed on with a local realtor. And he took a new nterest in Billy's paintings.

He even found a small loft to rent for Billy to set up a gallery nd studio, right downtown over one of the shops. So Billy was able o open his own gallery, just a couple of doors down from the dress hop where his mother worked.

Rachael had the most exciting news of all. It seems that a cus-omer of the dress shop, who bought one of Rachael's creations, wore hat dress to a convention in Los Angeles. A fashion writer for a California magazine spotted it and asked for a couple of photographs.

Well, a dressmaker in California called Rachael and invited ier to come out to show some of her dress designs to an association of ›uyers for dress manufacturers.

Rachael, as you remember, used to love to travel. And here was n invitation to show her own dress creations at a fashion show in California, all expenses paid. She was so excited when she got the call hat she ran over to Billy's studio.

"Billy, you won't believe this," Rachael shouted as she burst nto Billy's otherwise quiet and peaceful studio. "I'm just ecstatic!"

Sunrise At Two Lions

Enlightenment

A journey to
This mountain top
Cannot stop
To be explained
It must be experienced
First hand to comprehend
Any frame of reference
Will make no difference
If you find this
Story appealing
If it stirs some
Ineffable feeling
Of a majestic afternoon
A sky blue clarity
Of warm glowing charity
Your heart will do the rest
This time spent is
Meant to be
A gentle reminder
Of when you first found her
And calls you
To encouragement
On this journey of
Enlightenment

e n l i g h t e n m e n t

Chapter Seventeen – Enlightenment

They threw a little surprise party at the dress shop to congratulate Rachael and to wish her success on her trip. Billy showed up with a gorgeous bouquet of flowers and a card that he wrote and designed especially for the occasion.

The women in the shop were just giddy with excitement. The owner of the shop beamed with pride that someone from her shop had received this kind of recognition. The other two women were like giggly teenagers. And Rachael regained a glow and posture much more like the Rachael they all knew when she was a schoolgirl. It seemed like overnight, she looked ten years younger.

When Billy came in, it was his mother's turn to beam with pride. She took Billy by the arm and walked him around to say hello to the owner of the shop and the other two women who worked with her.

As Billy and Rachael approached the table where the snacks and punch were set up, another young woman came out from the dressing room.

"Oh, Billy, I don't think you've met our newest..." Rachael started to say.

Billy couldn't believe his eyes. He must be wrong. It couldn't be. A part of Billy hesitated in disbelief, but the more excitable part took over and spoke first.

"Anna?" Billy heard himself say. He was expecting to b embarrassed by a confused look from this beautiful young woma who had just appeared before him. Or she could simply say, "Yes Well, that is exactly what she did.

"Yes," was all she said, simply and sweetly.

"You know Anna?" Rachael said, an obvious surprise in he voice. "Anna just moved here from Boothbay Harbor. I didn't kno you two had met."

This was Anna from the castle, the same Anna who used t bring Billy apple pie when they were at that mystical castle together long time ago.

It was the same grown up Anna who opened the door to gree Billy when he paid that brief visit back a few months ago, and sa Nana there.

The other people at Rachael party, and especially Rachae must have thought that Anna and Billy were thunderstruck by eac other. They were, but not in exactly the way the others thought. Wel maybe not exactly. But Anna and Billy did feel a jolt from cupid arrow – no question about it.

For the next couple of hours, while the women in the sho talked excitedly about Rachael upcoming adventure, and how the couldn't wait for her to come back and tell them all about it, Anna an Billy couldn't take their eyes off from each other for more than a fe seconds at a time.

Finally Billy told his mother that he was going to walk Ann home. That announcement brought a coordinated wave of raised ey brows, secret glances and a chorus of tittering.

Before Billy and Anna left, Billy gave his Mom a big tight hu that lasted for a real long time. And they each had tears streamin down their faces when they finally pulled apart. Both Billy and Rachael knew why, without a word being exchanged between them.

"I didn't know if you were real. I mean I didn't know you were alive. I mean… I don't know what I mean," Billy sputtered.

"Me, too," Anna said.

They walked together toward Anna's apartment, located just a couple of minutes walk from downtown, without another word. As they walked up the front steps, Billy broke the ice.

He asked Anna to sit on the steps with him. Then he told Anna how he came to the castle, starting with the story of going ice fishing with his father. Anna listened silently as Billy began his story. When he came to the part about the two lions on the front steps, Anna spoke up.

"Wolfgang taught me about the lions."

"Wolfgang taught you about the lions?" Billy repeated. "William taught me about the lions."

"No, William did the paintings," Anna corrected.

Billy stopped her there. They started laughing and agreed that they needed to do a lot of talking about their experiences. Billy would ask if she met Jonathan or Aaron, and Anna would ask about Vincent and Jim or Cynthia.

As they rattled off the names, they found that they had met the same eleven other people, plus each other, at the castle. But the roles they played in each of their lives, while they were at the castle, were slightly different.

In the midst of this exchange, it occurred to Billy that he didn't know how Anna came to the castle. And he was still not sure about her or the other people there. When he asked, Anna told him a story that was in its detail, very different from Billy's.

Anna was ten years old, living in Boothbay Harbor with her

mother when it happened. She and her mother owned a bed and breakfast, and Anna loved helping her Mom prepare the breakfast and wait on the guests. Anna especially loved meeting and talking to all the interesting people who came to stay at their inn during the summer months.

Anna's mother would play the piano, an antique baby grand that sat in the front parlor, during the early evenings in the summer. The guests, many who had come back to the inn regularly for years, would come down to sit quietly and listen. Anna would sit out on the front porch, listen to the piano and swing gently in an old wooden glider.

One evening in late August of that year, one of the guests asked Anna's mother if he could play his violin along with her as she played the piano. She happily agreed and the other guests applauded as this man unpacked his beautiful violin.

Anna was in her usual spot out on the porch, dreamily swinging away. She had met the elderly man who asked to play, and he had seemed to be a very gentle and humble man. Anna immediately liked him. She waited with great anticipation to hear him play his violin while her mother played piano. She had no idea what was to come.

Anna's mother started with a piece of music that Anna recognized. It was one she had heard often, and enjoyed very much. She closed her eyes and allowed the pleasant tones of the piano to take her to that peaceful place inside.

Anna had found recently that if she focused her entire attention on the sound of the piano music and simply followed the rhythm of her breathing, she could shut off all thoughts and experience a uniquely peaceful feeling.

This beautiful and relaxing feeling had come to her out of nowhere one evening, while she was sitting especially still, swinging

ently in the warm evening breeze. It surprised her, in a very pleasant way. It was if she had tuned into another place in her awareness of reality. So now when she listened to the music, she listened very calmly, yet intently, anticipating the wonderful sensation of inner peace.

She would listen, thinking of nothing but the upcoming notes of the music, and simply tune in to her breathing. She would be aware of when she was inhaling and when she was exhaling, nothing more. She had found that this breathing exercise kept her mind from wandering as she listened to the music.

This was her favorite time of the day, a time she looked forward to every day. So as the music drifted into her consciousness she began to breathe gently and silently, knowing she would soon be transported to her peaceful place.

What she had not anticipated was the effect of the incredibly sweet and harmonious sounds of the violin as it blended with the piano. It felt to her as if a soothing balm was being applied to her forehead, taking her to that special inner world.

Anna relaxed more deeply than she ever remembered relaxing before, and within seconds she entered a world of splendor she had never experienced before. Here's how Anna told her story:

A soft blue light enveloped me, and I floated as if on a cloud. I could smell flowers more fragrant than any I had ever known. The aroma was so vivid that I could taste the flowers almost as if I were a hummingbird or a butterfly drinking in the nectar.

The music became even more beautiful with every passage. A joy began to fill my every cell until I thought I would burst out laughing. I would have if the incredible peacefulness within me had not been so soothing.

The soft blue light flashed brighter for a moment and then

turned to a pure white as I entered yet another dimension of this fantastic voyage.

In the midst of this white light, I knew that I had come into heavenly place. I felt that I was a part of heaven, yet known by heaven. I felt myself to be in God's presence.

And then, I found myself on the path to the castle. The ocean breeze blowing past the big house carried a refreshing spray that seemed to bring me out of my dreamlike state.

But it only seemed that way. I remained standing on the gently winding road, looking ahead at the castle on the edge of the ocean. A man with white hair approached and took me by the hand.

I recognized him as Wolfgang, the man who had asked to play the violin. He spoke to me by name and walked me toward the castle. I immediately felt safe and at ease.

"Do not pay any attention to the lions," he said as we started up the stairs to castle. I wasn't sure what he meant by this, but I would later learn.

At this point, Billy had to stop Anna. He was so enthralled with Anna's story that he could hardly breathe. It amazed him to hear such a different story, yet such a similar story.

Anna didn't fall through the ice and freeze, she was just listening to beautiful music. But they each described this beautiful light and used the same words to describe their experience. They came into the presence of God. That's how they both said it.

Billy asked Anna if she remembered when he came to the castle. She told him that he was already there when she came. She said she met a woman they called, "Nana", in the kitchen, and the first thing she did was ask Anna to take a piece of apple pie and a glass of milk up to Billy's room.

"That's when I met, you, Billy," Anna told him. "That's when saw all the beautiful paintings that William did."

"William did?" Billy said, very surprised to hear this. "William lidn't paint all those paintings. Different people at the castle painted hem."

"Nana told me that William painted them all." Anna said quietly.

Well, at this point to say that Billy was confused and filled with questions would be a huge understatement. He was flabbergasted. He started to ask about so many things that Anna just stopped him.

She told Billy that he was asking logical and rational questions, but their time at the castle was neither logical nor rational. Their experiences had nothing to do with time, or sequence of events. What had happened to them was beyond time and space, beyond what the rational mind can grasp. This is why so many people refuse to believe what happened to them, or are so frightened to even hear about it.

People tend to believe that we are nothing more than we can see and feel and think about, but there is more. She reminded Billy that they each had experienced this more. Billy acknowledged with another bob of the head, but he kept quiet for the moment.

Anna went on to say things to Billy that he already knew and agreed with on every point. But he didn't stop her, because he loved hearing the affirmation of what he already knew.

They both knew that the problem is, that what happened to hem has to be experienced to be believed. It cannot be explained precisely. It can only be alluded to by analogy or metaphor, or told as an allegorical story. And Anna had a pretty good vocabulary for doing just that.

It didn't matter what season of the year it seemed to be. Didn't he remember that everyday it was warm and beautiful? Didn't he remember the awesome sunrises every morning? Didn't he feel brand new every morning?

Anna just kind of smiled watching Billy' head bob up and down with each rhetorical question. Anna asked him to listen to rest of her story, and told him that they would have plenty of time to talk.

As I said, when William and I came into the castle, we came into a big and warm kitchen, where I could smell apple pie cooking. Wolfgang introduced me to Nana, and later I met William and the other people out on the porch.

Billy recalled that he had never seen or met the woman they called Nana. He had only seen his real Nana when he had that vision of returning briefly to see her there, after the accident, when she died.

Anna listed the names of the people she met on the porch, and Billy heard the familiar names. But his mind took him back to that recollection of never meeting the Nana at the castle. Anna noticed that he was off somewhere and cleared her throat. Billy snapped back to attention, and she continued:

My room was a big room, with natural wood beams and walls. The texture and grain of the wood was so interesting and beautiful that I used to spend time just looking at the variations while I listened to the music that Wolfgang would talk about.

Every day we would spend hours listening to music. Wolfgang would talk about the music and how music could open doors of perception that were beyond what most people even imagined. He would talk about a piece of music and how it was capable of transporting us o a heavenly place.

Somehow, every time he would finish telling about how a particular piece of music was meant to be appreciated by more than just our ears, music would begin to play. I don't know where it came from, or how it would just begin. But it happened every time he spent time with me. He would tell me to let the music take me with it to a magical place.

And I could hear the music throughout the house every day. I could even hear it as I walked along the beach with William or with Cynthia, or Karen. It was incredibly beautiful and peaceful. I just floated when I listened to it in the way that Wolfgang taught me to listen.

He would tell me to empty my mind of thoughts of the day, as I watched the sunrise every day, and to listen to the music in my mind. He taught me to feel the different sounds of the music creating the ever-changing colors in the morning sky.

I would listen to the stringed instruments and watch as the sounds seemed timed perfectly with beams of light in the morning sky that would streak out in brilliant gold and bright reds.

The percussion sounds would cause the pastel clouds to billow. And as the sounds softened, the colors in the sky would soften, until the sky became absolutely clear and blue.

Wolfgang called this time in the morning, the sunrise of the heart. He said it was the most beautiful way to start the day, and suggested that I should do this every day. And so I did.

When Wolfgang would talk to me about Furman and Dunbar…

Now that was too much for him. Billy had to interrupt.

"Furman and Dunbar," he all but shouted. "I haven't even

thought about those names for years and years. He kept saying the names over and over and shaking his head.

"Those are the lions of fear and doubt," Anna offered.

"I know. I know," Billy laughed. "I'm sorry. Go on with your story. You're so beautiful. I mean, your story is so beautiful."

And so Anna went on to tell Billy about how Wolfgang taught her to softly hum the music she was so familiar with, whenever the lions would try to discourage her or frighten her away from the castle.

When she would hum, even just to herself, they would go absolutely silent and lay down on their paws.

She told Billy that the lions would tell her that everyone would call her crazy if she spoke about her time at the castle. Anna noticed Billy's now familiar nod of acknowledgement. And as Anna told Billy more and more times of the lions and what Wolfgang said about them, he could hear the same words he had heard from William.

Finally Anna told Billy that after a time that seemed like months, she opened her eyes.

Come to find out, Anna had fallen asleep on the porch swing and spent the night there. Everyone inside was so taken with the music of the piano and violin that they all, including Anna's mother, forgot about Anna on the porch.

Anna woke up as the early morning sun hit her eyes. She could still hear the music and thought for a moment that she still at the castle. But she was home with her mother.

Now she hadn't been missing for months like Billy had been. She had just slept overnight. But to her it seemed like months. Remember when Billy broke through the ice, he thought he had just been under the water for a few minutes. So Anna was certainly right about the time not being real.

Enlightenment

The experience they shared was real. Billy was eager to tell
Anna about his teachings, and how William taught him about the
lions, and what happened with Sharon kissing the lions on the forehead. But before he could get started, he and Anna realized that it was
beginning to get light out. They had talked all night. They kind of
both realized it at the same time, and stood up together.

"Oh, my God. I've got to be at piano practice by nine," Anna
said. "I've got to go."

And with that, she ran into the house. Billy strolled, almost
floated back to his studio. He had a sofa there, and an afghan that
Nana made for him when he was young. Whenever he would get
engrossed in a new painting, which happened often, and work late
into the night, he would curl up on the sofa. cover himself with Nana's
afghan, and sleep at the studio.

Now Billy had been up all night talking with Anna. So you
would have thought that he would stumble into the studio, flop down
on the sofa and be asleep in seconds. But it didn't happen that way.

Billy had painted eleven paintings from the castle experience.
He hadn't really thought about it, but there was one more painting. It
flashed into his mind when he walked into the studio. Maybe this
time with Anna had something to do with it.

The gallery was filled with about fifty or sixty paintings of
seascapes and landscapes. Billy had even done a few portraits on commission. He hadn't really received any particular notice as a young
artist, but he had a local reputation as being a pretty talented artist.
And, like most artist, just a little strange.

The past summer he had traveled with a group of artists who
go from town to town along the coast of Maine, setting up outdoor
art shows.

With all the vacationers in Maine in the summer, the shows

are well attended, and some of the artists make enough money in th summer to spend the rest of the year painting and replenishing thei artwork.

At the first show Billy joined, he set up his mobile gallery o wire and wood, topped with a light tarp in case of rain, and hun about thirty paintings. He had experimented with watercolor an liked the soft pastel effects and "happy accidents" that add an energ and liveliness to watercolors sometimes. He liked the way they juxta posed his startling intense acrylics. So he had quite a variation o paintings to show.

Much of his work was in the abstract, free style that he enjoye painting. But he had a few realistic paintings in the more tradition style of New England barns, and bridges and majestic landscapes. Hi seascapes were all in the semi-abstract, depending-on-who's-looking at-them, style.

After Billy set up his presentation at this first outdoor show, h decided to take a stroll along the street to meet some of the othe artists, and take a look at the different styles of artwork. He was mor than a little surprised.

The veterans of these shows had come to know what sells an what doesn't. Billy's paintings were mostly in the what-doesn't catego ry. Almost all of the work he saw was of traditional nostalgic Main scenes.

There were beautifully painted flowers in a kind of Main meadow mode, and a few unusual approaches to painting flowers. Bu booth after booth boasted Maine traditions. Sailboats, landscape seascapes, barns, sailboats, seascrapes, landscrapes, barns, on and on.

Billy had even brought the eleven paintings that he had creat ed from his time at the castle. These were definitely in a class by them selves. And if Billy was worried that he might have to part with then is worries were groundless.

Oh, a few people liked them, especially very young kids and ery elderly people. Mostly they were ignored, and people tended to urry along past Billy's show. He didn't sell a painting at his first show.

By the second show, Billy had acquiesced to the tourist's taste, nd his show was now mostly traditional Maine scenes, with a few atercolors that were still slightly impressionistic.

He had worked with a passion, painting two or three paintings day, and even getting up in the night often to paint another one or wo before daylight. He could be pretty prolific as a painter, like most ainters who get hungry can be.

So he sold a few paintings at the second show, and a few more t the third. By the end of the summer, he had made enough sales to ee him through much of the winter.

He lived at home with his grandfather and his expenses were ninimal. His grandfather even subsidized a good portion of his studio ent, though Billy didn't know it. Grampa had told him that the wner of the building was an old friend, and had given him a super leal on the rent. At least Billy was surviving as an artist. Not many do.

As he walked into the studio that night, or rather that early norning, after being up all night, he glanced up at his private collec-ion of those eleven paintings that he had decided never to sell.

That was kind of a private joke with himself. He doubted that nyone would ever buy them, anyway. But he made this facetiously olemn vow that he would never sell these paintings that were inspired y his time at the castle.

Anyway, he looked at them and suddenly remembered the welfth painting. And even more startling to him was the clear recol-ection that it was Anna who talked to him about this painting. As sual, the words popped into his vision, and he wrote them down.

Enlightenment

A journey to
This mountain top
Cannot stop
To be explained
It must be experienced
First hand to comprehend
Any frame of reference
Will make no difference
If you find this
Story appealing
If it stirs some
Ineffable feeling
Of a majestic afternoon
A sky blue clarity
Of warm glowing charity
Your heart will do the rest
This time you've spent is
Meant to be
A gentle reminder
Of when you first found her
And calls you
To encouragement
On your journey of
Enlightenment

The twelfth painting appeared in the usual fashion of the other eleven. Billy painted actively, but calmly. He had no conscious thought of selecting color or position of the brushstrokes.

As Billy painted, the warm colors of the morning sun began to streak across his room, in contrast to the cool colors of the painting. As soon as the painting was done, Billy literally fell onto the sofa and slept soundly until around noon.

At noon he got up and walked over to the diner for a late breakfast. Billy enjoyed the people at the diner, and having a casual breakfast was one of his favorite indulgences.

Breakfast at the diner was always a kind of reward Billy gave himself for selling a painting, or getting a commission, or making good progress on a painting. Truth was, he rewarded himself with breakfast at the diner without any rationale at all. He enjoyed going for breakfast, and the people at the diner always enjoyed seeing him come in.

Billy was thinking, and half-kidding to himself, that he must look awful. He hadn't slept all night, except for a few hours on his studio sofa this morning, hadn't showered, and hadn't changed his clothes. So when he heard what Betty, the owner of the diner, said as she poured his customary big glass of orange juice, he was surprised.

"Well, aren't we just glowing this morning. That's the brightest smile I've seen from you in a while. You got a new girlfriend or something?"

Seems Billy wasn't the only intuitive one in town. He laughed and said that he thought he must have looked a fright, he had stayed up all night and hadn't even been home to shower.

"Could have fooled me," Betty said. Just about the time she got that out of her mouth, she spotted someone else coming into the diner and spoke to her.

"How'd the piano lesson go, young lady?"

When Betty looked at Anna, as she asked her about the piano lesson, she caught Anna's expression. Anna was looking at Billy. Now, not much gets by the local diner staff and the regulars in a small town.

It took Betty about a split second to put two and two together. Billy and Anna; of course, that was the girl someone had seen Billy walking with yesterday. She had just starting taking piano lessons from Betty's aunt.

"I guess you know Billy," Betty said as she motioned for Anna to sit down across from Billy at his table. Anna obliged, nodded, and smiled at Billy. With that Betty walked back behind the counter and whispered something to one of her waiters.

Well, Anna and Billy had breakfast together, lunch together and Billy took Anna home to meet his grandfather. And Billy cooked dinner for Anna that evening.

Billy and Anna were inseparable from the time they met up at the diner that morning. If they weren't on the phone, they were talking at the dress shop or meeting at the diner. In the evening Billy was at Anna's listening to her play the piano, or they were at Billy's house where he would cook for her and serve her in the dining room.

One day, after a couple of weeks had gone by, Anna knocked on the door to Billy's studio. She had never been in, even though they talked about it. Anna was either working or practicing piano or at a piano lesson. She would meet Billy at the diner or at his house, but this was her first visit to his art studio.

When Billy opened the door, he was surprised and happy to see Anna standing there. He smiled and reached out to give her a hug but she looked right past him. Anna saw the row of the twelve paintings. This time it was she who was absolutely thunderstruck. She managed to say Billy's name, but it was more of a croak than her usual sweet tone.

She floated over to the wall with the twelve paintings and just stared at one and then the other for the longest time. When she turned to look at Billy, she had tears streaming down her face. She didn't say anything, she just walked over and put her arms around Billy and held on tightly.

Billy thought his heart would burst at that moment. With every second that he held Anna he could feel his love for her grow more tender and delightful. And just when he thought it was impossible to feel more intensely about her, she stepped back and recited the poem that went with the painting, *Enlightenment*. Only when she quoted the part about, "When you first found her," she said, "When you first found him."

As she said these words to Billy, he felt a connection with her that can only be called heavenly. In the next moment, while keeping his eyes on the beautiful Anna of twenty-three standing in front of him, he remembered the voice of a young girl of ten, telling him about this painting.

She was talking in almost a sing-song rhythm and he heard her talk about a love that would come into his life one day that would open his heart in such a way that nothing on earth could compare.

He had received those words, at the time, the way a ten-year-old boy would hear them. But now he heard them and felt the reality of their meaning deep within his heart. And suddenly he knew the meaning of the holy kiss in an entirely new light.

He knew that art and music could open the door to enlightenment and joy, and bring us to a level of consciousness where deep and abiding love dwells. He now knew of yet another very special way to open the door to this joy and peace beyond words. As he felt it and thought it, he heard Anna's young voice speak of it.

"*Billy, when we think of love,* we think of the feelings of tender caring, and all of those wonderful things. But there is a love that exceeds our most cherished dreams and expectations.

"The depth of this love between two people can go beyond the romantic love they feel for each other. Romantic love points the way, but there is a love that is heavenly.

"Billy, we have felt that love, the love that God has for us. We can feel that kind of love for other people when we are totally aware of God's love for us. This love I am speaking of is the pure and holy love that we felt when we came into God's presence, each in our own way. And it is the love we will feel for each other someday.

Billy opened his eyes and looked at Anna. She continued on her story of so many years ago, as if she were just talking about it a few minutes ago.

"When we were very young, we were shown a pathway to a special knowledge and understanding that few find. And now we have found a love for each other that is the most precious on earth.

"I have my music and you have your art. My heart is so filled with gratitude and appreciation. I am so humbled to have been shown this secret path, this sacred path. And now here I am with you.

"I love you. I love the paintings you have done, William King Fraser. Nana told me you would paint them all."

The end

Epilogue

Of course, that's not really the end of the story, but that's as far as the storyteller got before we pulled into South Station. I was left with a few questions, but I can pretty much imagine what happened.

Did Rachael ever come back from California? I don't think so. Did she return to her life of travel and great adventure? I hope so. I hope she dances, unafraid.

Did Billy and Anna marry and settle down in Maine? There's no question that they married. Where they are now? God only knows. But I bet wherever they are, there is a glow in the air for miles around, especially at sunrise and sunset. Are there lots of Billy's and Anna's in the world? Oh, yes. I'm quite certain of that. Did they really meet in some mystical castle, when they were youngsters or did they share some bizarre dream?

And is possible that Billy was really William, when he was young? How could that be? And who were the other people at the castle? Where did they come from, and where are they now? And were they real at all? Was this all a glimpse of heaven?

Maybe someday you or I will see someone, on a train or as the old song goes, across a crowded room, and they will tell us the rest of this story. In the meantime, I wish you peace and love and a fullness of joy beyond words. May you be given your own glimpse of heaven. If you're one of the fortunate ones who has already experienced that glimpse of heaven, may you be ever grateful and humble for receiving such a gift.

I am,

Jeff Belyea

Give a gift of **Sunrise At Two Lions** to your family, friends and colleagues. Check your local bookstore, order online at *www.mindgoal.com* or mail the order form. Please include $3.75 shipping for one book, and $1.75 for each additional book.

The Twelve Paintings in this book are also available as 11x17 artist-signed posters at $29.95 each plus the same shipping charges as noted for the book. Include name and quantity of posters ordered. Maine residents please add sales tax. Please include check or money order for total, or furnish credit card information below.

Please send____copies of **Sunrise At Two Lions** @ $29.95 to:

Name_____

Organization_____

Address_____

City/State/Zip_____

Credit card _____ card #_____

Expiration date_____

Signature_____

Poster order:

Name of painting_____ Quantity_____

Name of painting_____ Quantity_____

Name of painting_____ Quantity_____

Fax (207)879-0314

SuiteOne Design Group
P.O. Box 574
Portland, Maine 04112
1-800-330-4975 • www.suiteonedesign.com